Dead of Night

A play

Peter Whalley

Samuel French – London
New York – Sydney – Toronto – Hollywood

DEAD OF NIGHT

First presented at the Liverpool Playhouse by arrangement with Brian Kirk on 23rd August, 1989, with the following cast:

Jack	Philip Madoc
Maggie	Jackie Lye
Dennis	Geoffrey Hughes
Lynne	Sally Watts

Directed by Ian Kellgren
Designed by Elroy Ashmore
Lighting design by Leslie Lyon

CHARACTERS

Jack
Maggie
Dennis
Lynne

The action of the play takes place in the living-room of
Jack's house, somewhere in England

ACT I   Late at night
ACT II   Immediately after

Time—the present

ACT I

The living-room of a house, somewhere in England. It is late at night

French windows to the back overlook an overgrown garden. The hallway is off to the left. The kitchen to the right. The furniture is second-hand verging on antique

The room is in darkness. Outside is a starry sky and silence. We hear a car drawing up and stopping close by. Car doors. Then the front door being unlocked and opened. For a few seconds there is the warning bleep of a burglar alarm before it is silenced

Maggie enters. She is an attractive woman in her mid-twenties. She proceeds to switch on the lights and draw the curtains. She has the air of someone relieved to have reached the end of a long and trying day

Jack follows her into the room. He is an imposing man in his forties. Like Maggie, he is smartly dressed. He gazes round the room as though seeing it for the first time. He nods and smiles as though in grateful recognition of his being there

Jack The innocent man returns to the scene of his crime.

Maggie (*amused*) Something like that.

Jack No, it's good to be home. 'Specially when you consider the alternative. Thank Christ there's still justice to be had in this land of ours. Also to be had—is a drink. What would you like?

Maggie Well, just a titchy brandy then.

Jack (*serving drinks for them both; in the style of Tom Jones*) "Then I awake and look around me ... At the four grey walls that surround me ..."

Maggie Oh, please ... !

Jack   "I realize that I was only dreaming.
                For there's a guard, and there's a sad, old padre.
                On and on we'll walk at daybreak
                Again I'll touch the green, green grass of home."

Cheers.

Maggie Cheers.

Jack Listen, let me ask you something. Serious question.

Maggie Then you should have asked it before we got on to the champagne.

Jack No, no ... what would you have done if I'd been sent down?

Maggie What would I have done ... ?

Jack Yeah, would you, you know—the old cliché—would you have waited for me?

Maggie Come on, Jack ...

Jack Well, would you? I'm interested.

Maggie For how long?

Jack Oh say ... five years. Ten ...

Maggie No.

Jack (*taken aback*) No?

Maggie No.

Jack Ah. Good job I wasn't then.

Maggie Well, you wouldn't have wanted me to. You would have said forget about me, don't waste your life.

Jack Well, I might have done, yes. Now you mention it. (*Then, with fist raised in triumph*) Ha! We did it! Did it, did it, did it! (*Then*) And, credit where credit's due, that barrister wasn't such a twat as I first thought.

Maggie He was good. I told you he was.

Jack It was just his, you know, his manner. I mean he was a twat really. (*Then*) Why wouldn't you let that photographer take your picture?

Maggie The one from *The Star*.

Jack *The Star*, yeah.

Maggie groans

He wasn't asking you to take your dress off. He just wanted one of me and you together. Happy couple celebrating. It would have been nice.

Maggie I couldn't stand him. Or that reptile of a reporter. Now he would have liked me to have taken my dress off.

Jack Hmm. Still, he should give me a good spread. From the way he was talking. It's not just going to be your two-inch column job. I'm going to be the biggest thing in that newspaper without tits.

Maggie I don't doubt.

A pause

Jack My old dad was up in court once.

Maggie Yes?

Jack Drunk-and-disorderly. I don't know what he got but it was nothing to the earache my mother gave him afterwards. It was the women who kept the peace then, you know.

Maggie You've never told me anything about your parents.

Jack (*shrugging*) Not a lot to tell. They survived. That was their achievement. Dad was a rag-and-bone merchant.

Maggie Oh, I see.

Jack Where I get it from, yeah. I used to go round with him. Dishing out the pumice-stones. You know, call me a sentimental old fool if you like, but in those days the world was full of wonderful people.

Maggie Still is.

Jack No. There was a time—which you're too young to have known but there was a time—when they sang hymns before the Cup Final at Wembley. A football crowd sang hymns. Can you believe that? I mean where did we lose it? What is it that's changed?

Maggie People can still be wonderful.

Jack (*admitting*) That jury, they were wonderful. God bless their little cotton socks, every one of 'em.

A pause

Maggie When they went out . . .
Jack Yeah?
Maggie What did you think? Did you think they might find you guilty
or . . . ?
Jack Didn't know. I really didn't know. And my brief didn't have much of
a clue either. He came down to the cell. Keep me company. Ha. I'd have
got more company out of a dead frog. But anyway. I said so, what do you
think then? And he's on the one hand this . . . and the other hand that . . .
Like the twat that he was. It was a sickener for that judge though. He'd
have had me hung, drawn and quartered, no question. He had that crazed
look in his eye. Trickle of saliva coming from the corner of his mouth . . .
Maggie He was an ordinary judge.
Jack Exactly.

Maggie is amused

I bet he's still got his little black cap from when they used to hang 'em.
Keeps it all nice and pressed in a drawer at home, hoping some day he'll
be able to use it again. Well, not on me, sunshine! You missed your
chance with me! (*Then*) Actually, when you think about it, this whole
case—this verdict—it could turn out to be a . . . you know, what's that
French word?

Maggie makes a gesture of helplessness

A special case, a special cause . . .
Maggie *Cause célèbre.*
Jack (*gesturing she's got it*) *Cause célèbre.* That's what it could well be when
the history of England comes to be written. A *cause célèbre.*
Maggie (*in amused protest*) When the history of England what? It's been
written already. Written a hundred times. Didn't they have any books
when you went to school?
Jack School? What makes you think I went to school?
Maggie Stupid of me.
Jack But, anyway, when they write this particular bit of the history of
England, then I think I might just come in for a mention.
Maggie These newspapers.
Jack What newspapers?
Maggie That are going to carry the story.
Jack Ah.
Maggie They won't give your address, will they? I mean our address, this
house . . . ?
Jack Why?

She shakes her head

You're frightened it might become a shrine? Or that we'll be over-run
with tourists wanting to know was this really where it happened and while
they're here would we mind if they used the lavatory?
Maggie It doesn't matter.
Jack No, no, I'm sure they won't. Though I still wish you'd let him take
that picture of us together. Let people see the woman that stood by me

through all this. Which I do appreciate. And I want you to know that. I mean it's been a difficult six months. Hell of a six months. This thing hanging over us like some great, black cloud. Blocking out everything. Daylight, everything. Stopping us thinking about anything else. Stopping me saying what I've been wanting to say. Which is that—I would like you to marry me.

She says nothing

Maggie?
Maggie Yes?
Jack Le's get married. Tie up the loose ends. Make an honest man out of me.
Maggie I don't ... I don't know.
Jack What is there to know? You know I love you. Yes?
Maggie Yes.
Jack Well, then.

Still she says nothing

Look, I know I'm not doing this right. I should have come with red roses and a ring in a little, padded box. It's just I've had quite a busy day one way and another. Look, I'll go down on my knees ... (*Which he does*)
Maggie Oh no, Jack don't ...
Jack I love you. I worship you. I adore you.
Maggie And I find you ridiculous like that. Will you get up please!
Jack No. I'm not going to move from here till you say yes.
Maggie Then you're going to end up deformed.
Jack I don't care. Wait, just let me hitch up my trousers. Don't want to spoil the suit. Marry me.
Maggie Look, I don't want to talk about it now. My head's just ... (*She gestures to suggest it's exploding*)
Jack Then say yes and we'll talk about it tomorrow. I swear I won't ever stand upright again till you say yes.

The doorbell rings

Shit.

Maggie laughs

Well, at least say yes so I can go and answer the door!
Maggie It won't be more reporters, will it?
Jack (*shaking his head*) Dennis and Lynne.
Maggie You think so?
Jack I rang them from the restaurant. Said if they wanted to call round, join in the festivities ...
Maggie (*mildly*) You might have told me.

The doorbell rings again

Jack Say you'll marry me.
Maggie No.

Jack You'd leave me on my knees . . . ?

Maggie They'll think you're drunk. They've seen you drunk before. They won't mind.

She goes out to answer the door

Jack thinks about it, then gets to his feet. As we hear off . . .

(*Off*) Hi. Come in . . .

Lynne (*off*) We were delighted, love, absolutely delighted.

Dennis (*off*) Don't worry. We're not stopping.

Lynne (*off*) And where is he then . . .

They enter with Maggie. Lynne is in her late thirties, casually dressed with a sunbed tan. Dennis is about the same age, as indifferent to his appearance as Lynne is particular about hers

(*Embracing Jack*) Jack . . . ! I'm so relieved, I am, honest.

Jack You and me both.

Dennis Congratulations, Jack. (*He shakes Jack's hand*)

Jack Thank you, Dennis.

Lynne You were on the news, you know. Have you seen it? National news tonight?

Jack Headlines was it? First on?

Lynne Well, no, but . . . (*She looks to Dennis*) Third or fourth . . . ?

Dennis shrugs

I mean it wasn't right at the end where they do something funny about the Royal Family or animals.

Maggie Don't encourage him. We've had the press hanging on to his every word all night.

Lynne And so they should be.

Jack This is the gutter press we're talking about here, Dennis.

Dennis What, you mean *The Daily Telegraph* . . .

Jack laughs. He motions to shoot him with his finger

Lynne (*embracing Maggie*) Oh, I'm so pleased for you both, I really am!

Maggie Thanks.

Jack So let's have a little drinkette, shall we. Lynne, what would you like, my love? Gin-and-tonic?

Lynne Please.

Jack And Dennis . . . ?

Dennis (*looking at his watch*) Well, are you sure? I mean we don't want to be . . .

Lynne We're not keeping you up, are we?

Jack Course you're not.

Lynne (*to Dennis*) You see.

Jack Anyway, this isn't a night for sleeping. This is a night for celebrating. Fireworks. Bonfires from coast to coast . . .

Dennis I'll have a beer then, please.

Jack Certainly.

Lynne And you must tell us all about the trial and everything. Oh, unless it's something you'd rather not talk about ... ?

Maggie I think you'll find he doesn't mind.

Lynne I had the radio on all day at the hospital. Local radio, you know. And when it came on the news—not guilty—I just stood and cheered. All my geriatrics thought I'd gone as ga-ga as what they were.

Jack Do you want ice, Lynne?

Lynne No, it'll be fine as it is. And have you been out celebrating?

Maggie We went for a meal at the Blue Danube.

Lynne Oh, nice. I'm always wanting him (*indicating Dennis*) to take me there.

As Maggie provides an ashtray

Thanks, love.

Dennis The jury weren't out long then?

Jack Just over an hour.

Lynne Well, God bless 'em, whoever they were.

Jack One beer.

Dennis Thanks.

Lynne I mean it's a wonderful system, the jury system. But you could just end up with twelve idiots, couldn't you, and then where would you be?

Jack It wasn't the jury that bothered me. Least of my worries. It was the professionals that made me wonder what sort of game I was in.

Lynne What, you mean the lawyers ... ?

Jack Yeah. The wig-and-gown brigade.

Dennis Why did they bother you?

Jack Their home territory, wasn't it. Their ball-park. Rest of us were just visiting proles. Take my defence counsel for example ...

Maggie Here we go.

Jack There was a man I just couldn't communicate with, not at all. Couldn't talk to him. Tell you the truth, I think he came from another planet. I think he was a Martian.

Maggie He was very capable. I don't know why you keep——

Jack Cold he was. Had eyes like a fish.

Dennis Won the case for you though, didn't he.

Maggie Exactly.

Jack So Martians make good barristers, I'm not denying that. I just have a strong suspicion he wasn't flesh-and-blood, that's all. And the prosecuting counsel, right ... ?

Lynne The other side.

Jack Other side. The one that was trying to nail me. Well, he was flesh-and-blood all right. Just hand-in-glove with the judge though, wasn't he!

Maggie Not really, no.

Jack Either they lived together or they were both Masons, I don't know.

Dennis Why do you say that?

Lynne Dennis ... !

Dennis What?

Lynne You weren't even there.

Dennis I know I wasn't. Which is why I'm asking Jack why he thinks they were both Masons.

Jack There was this sort of understanding between them. Right there in the middle, where I was, you could feel it.

Dennis But they still found you not guilty.

Jack The jury did.

Dennis Well, yes, I mean ...

Jack The jury. Twelve men and true. 'Cept some of 'em were women. (*To Maggie*) Sorry, I didn't offer you, did I.

Maggie No, I'm all right.

Jack OK. Listen, anybody wants another drink, just help yourselves, all right?

Lynne We will.

Dennis looks at his watch

Jack (*pouring himself another drink*) So there I was, being defended by an alien being, possibly robotic, and prosecuted by the president of the local Masonic Lodge.

Maggie We get the picture.

Jack And the judge, well ... !

Maggie Jack wasn't over-keen on the judge.

Jack He wasn't over-keen on me. (*To Lynne*) I'll tell you what ...

Lynne What?

Jack Have you counted your geriatrics recently? You're sure there hasn't been one absent-without-leave this past week?

Lynne Well, they're all absent mentally to one degree or another.

Jack But no actual empty bed?

Lynne Not as I've noticed.

Jack Then it must be a different hospital he'd escaped from. Because he definitely wasn't *compos mentis*, this judge. I mean you wouldn't have sent him on a train journey without putting a label round his neck in case he got lost. What he really needed was sheltered accommodation and an alarm button. Mind, perhaps the Masons do supply such things, I don't know.

Maggie (*in amused protest*) I thought you were telling me he was a hanger and flogger ...

Jack Yes.

Maggie Desperate to be able to use his black cap again.

Jack He was. Probably what keeps him alive is that.

Dennis I'd have thought most judges were of your political persuasion.

Jack So would I. But we didn't get a chance to talk politics, did we. In his eyes ... his watery, pink, little eyes ... I was the accused. Which meant the guilty. Which meant he was furious I was wasting his time pleading not guilty. I mean if it hadn't been for me keeping him in court he could have been at home raising Dobermann pinschers or working on his Child's Guide to Capital Punishment.

Lynne It wasn't a long trial though was it. I mean I was surprised at how quickly——

Jack Yeah, well, there were very few witnesses, weren't there. They weren't needed. That was the whole point.

Dennis No dispute as to the facts.

Jack Absolutely.

Dennis Just the question of how the law was to be applied with regard to those facts.

Jack And whether I was going to be thrown into the nick for the next ten or fifteen years.

Dennis Well yes.

Jack I think that's what made it interesting for me really.

Lynne So what happened, Jack? Come on, give us a proper story.

Jack What happened. Right. Court's convened.

Lynne Yes.

Jack I'm charged. Manslaughter of Philip James Mercer ... da-da-da ... on January whatever-it-was ... How do I plead? Not guilty.

Lynne Because you weren't.

Jack Judge looks at me in disgust. He knows I'm lying. Anyway, jury's selected, sworn in, and the whole band-wagon starts to roll.

Lynne Is that when they say call the first witness?

Jack Well, pretty soon, yeah.

Lynne And who was it?

Jack Oh, some policeman. PC ... I don't know. PC Plod.

Lynne Call PC Plod.

Jack Call PC Plod.

Lynne Call PC Plod.

Jack PC Plod takes the stand. Now he's been called because he was first on the scene. First here. So he tells about how he found the body and what he observed. Which wasn't a lot. Basically me and this room and all that. And then my brief, the robotic Martian, he stands up and he wants to know who called the police in the first place.

Lynne Who did?

Jack I did.

Lynne Well, yes, I thought you did.

Jack Point in my favour. I didn't try to cover things up or flee the country. Course, as far as the judge is concerned, this only shows how cunning I am. He looks at me and he starts tapping on his desk with this big hook he has where one of his hands is missing ...

Maggie He had not! He had two quite normal hands.

Jack Perhaps I did imagine that bit.

Maggie No perhaps about it.

Jack Anyway, then, er ... well, there was a certain amount of discussion about what time my phone-call was logged and what time the police arrived. Judge is writing it all down, asking for things to be repeated. Takes out his ear-trumpet ...

Laughter

Then PC Plod also informs us that the deceased was identified as Philip Mercer, aged twenty-one.

Maggie Twenty-two.

Jack Well, whatever. The important thing being that he had a record for burglary as long as your arm. I mean we're not just talking opportunist here. We're talking about a career. Man with a vocation. Anyway, all this took time to get sorted. And of course lunch-breaks have to be strictly observed, because you can't have the local wine-bars going out of business. Back in the afternoon, slightly pissed, then adjourn again at half-four, which I imagine is opening-time down the Masonic Lodge.

Dennis There must have been some other prosecution witnesses? No?

Jack (*nodding*) William Fredrick Shawcross.

Maggie The pathologist.

Lynne Oh yes! Yes, I know him. Well, not socially, but I've come across him at the hospital.

Jack Yeah, well, so had I. He's been in the shop. Bought a pair of Chinese vases from me. Well, strictly speaking Italian, but Chinese in style. And a few other things, some of which were quite genuine.

Dennis And what did he have to say?

Jack Oh, results of post mortem. Deceased had been shot in the left thorax ... (*To Lynne*) Thorax?

Lynne (*nodding*) Chest.

Jack Right. Shot in the left thorax. This, in William Fredrick's opinion, was the cause of death. Which, in my opinion, I think was a fairly safe diagnosis. Probably one of his better ones. Then the Masonic prosecutor weighs in. He wants to know was there any bruising to other parts of the body. Well, there was a lot of arguing about this ...

Lynne But why though?

Dennis To establish how much of a fight there'd been. (*To Jack*) I imagine?

Jack You know, you'd have made a good barrister, you would, Dennis.

Dennis Is that a compliment or an insult?

Jack Oh, well, if you don't know that, then perhaps you wouldn't have made such a good barrister after all. (*He laughs*) But yeah, absolutely. Establish how much of a fight there'd been. So, anyway, my brief weighed in—Doctor Spock—he weighed in and they argued about bruising for a good hour or two. Except they didn't call it bruising ...

Lynne Lividity.

Jack Lividity.

Lynne And I wasn't even there ... !

Jack Though personally, call it what you like, I couldn't see much point to any of it, save that I suppose it increased everybody's fees. Then the next witness ...

Lynne Call the next witness.

Jack That was another copper.

Lynne Call another copper.

Jack Can't remember his name but he was a firearms expert.

Lynne Call a firearms expert.

Jack And he testified that the bullet that killed Philip Mercer—Exhibit A, which he has in a little plastic bag—had been fired by Exhibit B. Which he has in another plastic bag. And Exhibit B, he says, is a Smith-and-Wesson hand-gun of nineteen fifties' manufacture. OK, so jury has a look at both exhibits, pass 'em round. No objections from Doctor Spock. Masonic man asks were there any identifiable prints on the gun—the gun being Exhibit B. Firearms expert says yes. Sets belonging to dead man, Philip Mercer and sets belonging to the accused, Jack Lilley. No objections. Everybody happy with all that. So the firearms expert steps down and I'm called to take the stand.

Lynne Did you have to take an oath?

Jack (*nodding*) Bible in my hand. I swear to tell the truth, the whole truth and nothing but the truth.

Lynne So help me God.

Jack No.

Dennis They only say that in the States.

Jack Right.

Lynne Oh.

Jack Of course now I'm in the witness-box, right? Which is up close next to the judge. And he's looking at me as though to say don't forget I've still got my little black cap at home.

Maggie Now who's telling the truth and nothing but the truth?

Jack Well, unless I got him wrong, I don't know. Perhaps he was waiting for me to bung him a few quid and that's what put his back up when I didn't.

Lynne You don't get many women judges, do you.

Maggie You don't, no.

Jack Listen, don't you think I had enough problems . . .

Maggie gives a cry of protest

Anyway, anyway, my brief says will I give an account of what happened on the night of Jan. twenty-first in my own words.

Lynne Well, go on!

Jack You know it. You've heard it before.

Lynne Not what you said in court we haven't!

Jack I just said—I was sitting here in my own home. In that chair as a matter of fact. Let's call it Exhibit C, right? I was sitting in Exhibit C. It was very late. About this time, come to think of it. A dark night. Maggie had gone to bed. Oh, at which I get another glance from His Honour since this suggests immorality of a high order, us not being married. Worth at least a flogging. But, anyway, on the night in question I'm sitting in Exhibit C, with just the one light on.

Lynne Exhibit D.

Jack Right. Rest of the house is locked up and in darkness. And why am I sitting here? Well, no mystery. Just because I'm not really tired. I've got all sorts going through my head about the shop and one thing and another.

Lynne I get like that sometimes.

Jack Then, I hear a movement. Out there somewhere back of the house. And I know straightaway there's somebody out there. So I switch off the light. Pitch darkness. And I wait. And as my eyes begin to get used to the dark, I see that door start to open. Very slowly. And then a figure appears. And I'm sitting in this chair, thinking Christ, what do I do now? Then there's this figure. He switches on a torch. Just shines it on the floor, checking where he's going. And I'm thinking, well, it's now-or-never time. And I'm trying to remember from when we did unarmed combat in Aldershot twenty-five years ago. Can't remember a thing. So I just take a deep breath and switch the light back on.

Lynne (*in alarm*) Ah . . . !

Jack And I see this young man. Looking scared to death. Terrified. Mind, I probably looked scared to death as well. *So* we're standing here, looking scared to death at one another. And I said—stop there. Drop the torch. Hoping I might sound like I knew what I was doing. And I must have done, because he drops the torch. And I'm thinking—what the hell do I do now? And I thought—I actually remember thinking this—I thought at least he's smaller than me. But then he starts messing around in his pocket, trying to pull something out, and I realized what he's trying to pull out—it's a gun. He's got a gun and he's trying to pull it out of his pocket. I mean never mind he's smaller than me—he might be a three-foot midget—a gun makes him a giant. Only he's having trouble getting it out of his pocket. Because it's one of these nylon jackets and it's got caught up. So I manage to land a punch on him that puts him down on the floor. And I'm down on top of him, trying to grab this gun. We're both pulling at it. And it comes away in my hand and . . . well, I pull the trigger. Shoot him. Then I stand up. And he's lying there, looking more surprised than anything. And then he died.

A pause

Lynne It must have been like a nightmare.

Jack Was a bit. Anyway, after I've told 'em all this, the Masonic prosecutor starts coming on strong, wanting to know why I pulled the trigger. I wasn't claiming it was an accident, was I? I said no, I wasn't. So I must have intended it? I said I suppose I must have, but not intended as in thought about or planned. But I knew what I was doing? I say yes, I knew what I was doing but I didn't know I was going to do it. So we're going round in circles. If I knew what I was doing I must have meant to do it. Till I don't honestly know what I meant or what I thought or . . . (*He shakes his head*)

Lynne You mustn't blame yourself.

Maggie No.

Jack I don't as a matter of fact.

Lynne I mean it was his own fault, wasn't it. He broke in. He brought the gun with him. I still don't understand why they had to take you to court at all.

Dennis Because there was a case to be answered.

Lynne What case?

Dennis Manslaughter. Technically at least, it was possible manslaughter.

Jack Quite right, quite right.

Lynne Well, technically be buggered. I don't see it.

Jack Well, see, Lynne, what I should have done—if I understand His Honour's summing-up correctly—what I should have done ... I should have disarmed the aforementioned Mr Mercer and then, making sure he was in the best of health, I should have kept him here and informed the authorities, who would have arrived two hours later. And if he'd been hungry then I could have made him some supper. Given him a drink. Shown him round the house while we were waiting. I mean this is what His Honour the geriatric more or less said when he came to direct the jury. Oh, and when I say direct—I mean direct 'em to find me guilty.

Maggie No, he didn't. He just spelt out the letter of the law. No more, no less.

Dennis Which talks about reasonable force, doesn't it? You're entitled to use minimum reasonable force, or something on those lines ... ?

Maggie Yes.

Lynne But what's minimum reasonable force against a man with a gun?

Dennis He didn't have a gun though, did he. Jack had taken it off him.

Jack You're not related to this judge by any chance are you, Dennis? I mean he's not your father or——

Maggie (*checking him*) Jack ...

Jack Only joking.

Lynne I mean the fact he was carrying the gun meant he was threatening Jack's life, wasn't he?

Dennis In a way.

Lynne So that gives Jack the right to defend himself.

Dennis Yes, but not necessarily to kill the man.

Lynne It gives you the right to do to him whatever he was going to do to you!

Dennis No.

Jack Well, we spent about half a day on this, of course. I mean this was the crux.

Dennis It would be.

Jack I had it thrown at me from all angles by my Masonic friend. He seemed to think the first thing I should have done when I saw this character pulling a gun on me was to have said, er, do you mind just holding it there while I pop down the library and consult a few books on just what my rights are in this situation? Then come back and say, look, library's closed just now. Do you think we could leave this whole thing till tomorrow afternoon?

Lynne Ridiculous.

Jack Or I suppose I could have stood there and let *him* shoot *me*. Died with a clear conscience and no charge to answer.

Maggie They wanted to know why you didn't just use the gun to frighten him off or keep him there or——

Jack Because it wasn't like that!

Maggie Well I know but——

Jack It was the middle of the night. I was fighting for my life. He was going to kill me and so when I got the chance to kill him ... bang.

Dennis Were there any more witnesses?

Jack No. No more witnesses, no. There was just the, you know, summings-up. First of all Doctor Spock tells it like it is. Self-defence, all that. Then the prosecution tries to make out I'm some sort of psychopath. And that I have to be found guilty in order to deter all other potential psychopaths who're likely to find armed burglars bursting in. Like if they don't find me guilty, they're likely to have a rash of armed-burglar-killings on their hands. Then finally His Honour the geriatric lays the law down. Which basically is that they should forget everything they've heard and find me guilty. And if they don't they'll be barred from the Masonic Lodge for life. And all the time he keeps giving me the hard stare. Shouldn't be surprised if he hadn't got that little black cap with him in his pocket. I think he was probably wondering if he dared put it on, just for a minute, so's we could all see what it looked like.

Dennis But they still found you not guilty.

Jack Well, yes.

Dennis Despite everything that . . .

Jack The jury! It was the jury that found me not guilty!

Lynne Of course they did.

Dennis You said we should help ourselves . . .

Jack Sure, sure . . .

Lynne Get me another G-and-T, will you, Dennis?

Dennis proceeds to get drinks during the next

Jack Jury's unanimous verdict. Which, of course the ancient and venerable old bastard on the bench didn't like one little bit. Oh no. Nearly stuck in his throat when he had to tell me I was a free man. Nearly choked him. But it was the common man who was on my side. Oh, and I don't mean just the jury. Public gallery as well. You should have heard the cheer that went up when they heard the verdict. (*To Maggie*) Yes . . . ?

Maggie There was some applause.

Jack Certainly was. Till the judge stopped it. Which of course, he would do. But what I'm saying is, apart from the professionals, who were only interested in the legal niceties and the size of their own fees, the public reaction was all for me!

Maggie Well, except . . . (*She stops*)

Jack Except what?

Maggie You know.

Jack Oh, what, that couple of loud-mouths . . .

Maggie Yes.

Jack (*to Dennis and Lynne*) Couple of loud-mouths in the public gallery. I hardly noticed but Maggie told me afterwards. Apparently, as soon as we got the verdict, they started yelling about how they were going to get me . . .

Lynne Really?

Maggie Till the judge had them thrown out.

Jack Ah yes, fine man the judge. Did I mention that?

Maggie I think they were Philip Mercer's family. The dead man's family.

Lynne Oh, well, that explains it then.

Maggie They'd been there the whole trial.

Jack Well, I'm sorry they felt cheated. Didn't get their pound of flesh. But you can't please all the people all the time, can you.

Lynne And they were actually threatening to . . . ?

Maggie Yes.

Jack What does it matter? Forget 'em. If they want me . . . well, OK, they know where I am.

Maggie Jack, don't even say that, please.

Jack All right. I'm sorry, I'm sorry. But let's forget about them. They're not important. What was important—and I'm sure Dennis will agree—was that the court upheld the right of a citizen to defend himself and his home, yes?

Dennis (*after hesitating*) On this occasion, yes.

Jack Now I might not be much of a historian. I've not had the time to be. I've been too busy earning a living. But I think that shows the way the wind's blowing. Right? I mean in this country as a whole. The way opinion's moving.

Dennis And what way is that?

Lynne Don't start.

Dennis I'm merely asking Jack what way he considers opinion to be moving.

Jack Well, towards self-defence. Self . . . self-reliance. Instead of turning to the state for everything all the time.

Dennis Look after number one.

Jack If you like.

Dennis And bugger everybody else.

Jack You sound as though you're not altogether in favour, Dennis.

Dennis Do I.

Jack Let me put it this way. There was a time in this country when men used to carry swords, yes? Shakespeare's time. Whenever that was. Men carried swords and knives and . . .

Maggie Well, sometimes. But so what?

Jack So there was a time when it was accepted you had the right to protect yourself. And what I'm saying is that that time is coming back. Like everything does sooner or later. You only have to sell antiques to know that.

Maggie I can't say I've seen anybody round here wearing a sword.

Jack No, not wearing swords. But beginning to realize they have to protect themselves. Protect their property. Protect their families.

Dennis Then everybody's an enemy.

Jack Potentially, yes!

Dennis No.

Jack You're an idealist, Dennis. You're an idealist and I'm a realist. That's the difference between us.

Lynne They issued all the nurses with those screech-alarms last year.

Jack Anyway, what's so wrong about wanting to defend yourself? Or defend what's yours? It's one of the most basic human instincts.

Dennis So is revenge, greed, jealousy. It doesn't make them right.

Jack Nothing to do with it. A man has a God-given right to defend himself. But like so many other things over the years, since Shakespeare's day, we've given up that right. We've said the state'll do it. The state'll look after me. I can sit on my arse. I'm not responsible anymore.

Dennis I should have thought it was more the state saying we can't have all these people wandering around wearing swords. They'll all end up killing one another.

Maggie Yes.

Jack And has it worked?

Dennis Has what worked?

Jack Is the crime rate going up or is it going down?

Dennis That's not the point . . .

Jack I'm asking a very simple question. Is it going up or is it going down?

Lynne Up.

Jack Thank you.

Lynne Any time.

Jack The crime rate is going up. And why? Because we don't defend ourselves. Because we sit on our arses and expect the state to do it for us.

Dennis Oh, for Christ's sake . . .

Maggie The law doesn't stop you defending yourself.

Jack What? They prosecuted me. Tried to put me away for doing it!

Maggie But they didn't put you away, did they.

Jack Not for want of trying. They only didn't manage it because the jury wouldn't kotow when they had the whip cracked over 'em. This is what I'm saying. The law is behind the times. It's out of step with the way ordinary people are thinking.

Dennis So what is it you're suggesting? Every home should have its little arsenal? Every house to have a moat and portcullis to deter intruders?

Jack Never mind whether I'm suggesting it or not. It's already happening.

Dennis Moats . . . ?

Jack Not moats but . . .

Dennis (*to Lynne*) We haven't got a moat, have we?

Lynne We haven't even got a fish-pond, though I've been after one for long enough.

Jack Look around you. There are burglar-alarms everywhere. Private estates . . . security guards. We're not far off what I'm talking about.

Dennis Well, all I can say—when we finally get there, when the world is finally re-created in your image, I wouldn't want to live in it.

Jack Why, you think yours is so much better?

Dennis Yes.

Jack With muggers and rapists and murderers?

Dennis No, with . . . with ideals and aspirations . . .

Maggie Hear, hear.

Dennis And hope.

Jack Oh, you can have them. I don't mind them. So long as you've got the fire-power to put 'em into effect.

Dennis I don't agree with you, Jack. I don't agree with one word you say.

Lynne So what's new?

Jack I see. Then let me ask you this then, Dennis. If you'd have been on that jury, you'd have found me guilty, would you?

Maggie (*checking him*) Jack.

Jack Would you?

Maggie I don't think that's a very fair question.

Jack Oh he can say yes. I don't mind.

Lynne Well, I do. You wouldn't have found Jack guilty, would you?

Dennis I wasn't on the damn jury.

Maggie No, so he didn't hear all the arguments, so how on earth can you expect him to answer that?

Jack I think he's answered it already.

Dennis (*moving to leave*) Yeah, well, that's my lot . . .

Jack (*stopping him*) Ah no. No, Dennis, you're not going . . .

Dennis It's late. Bloody early start.

Jack Dennis . . . old pal . . . come on. We've never agreed about anything, have we, you and me. All the arguments we've had. So why should this be any different. Maggie, how about some supper, eh?

Maggie Supper . . . ?

Jack Lynne, you'll stop for some supper?

Lynne I'll stop for anything, me. And I'm on a late tomorrow so——

Jack Great. So, Dennis, Dennis, sorry but you can't go. If you go now, I'll think I've offended you and I'll never forgive myself.

Dennis You've always managed to forgive yourself before.

Jack (*laughing*) I like it. I like it. We're old sparring-partners, yeah? Give one another a bit of a bloody nose from time, but no grudges. Now then, Maggie my love . . . some supper, yeah?

Maggie Are you serious after all you've eaten?

Jack I'm starving.

Maggie OK. I'll do some salmon sandwiches.

Maggie goes off to the kitchen

Jack It's the cut-and-thrust of intellectual debate, you see. Gives you an appetite when you're not used to it.

Lynne I'm supposed to be on a diet. No snacks, no alcohol.

Jack But tonight is a special occasion.

Lynne So was last night. And the night before that. Dennis, you couldn't do me a big favour, could you? Go round to our house and get me a fresh packet of fags from the top drawer of the sideboard.

He gives a groan of dismay. She urges

Go on.

Dennis Yeah, sure. Why not.

Lynne You're a love.

Dennis goes out

Lynne glances towards the kitchen

(*Keeping her voice low*) Have you gone off women altogether or has it just been me in particular?

Alarmed, Jack motions her to be quiet. He moves to the door through which Maggie has gone and pushes it closed, then comes back to Lynne

Jack (*quietly*) Look, this isn't exactly the best moment . . .
Lynne So when is? When did I last get a chance to see you by yourself?
Jack I know.
Lynne Months ago.
Jack Yes.
Lynne Just hold me, Jack, will you. Just hold me for a minute.

He gives a nervous glance at the door, then takes her in his arms

I was beginning to forget what you felt like.

She tries to kiss him but he steps away

Jack Lynne.
Lynne What?
Jack I've been under . . . well, you can't imagine what I've been under.
Lynne I know what I haven't been under.
Jack This case. I haven't been able to think about anything else. It's like my whole life's been put on ice. Like I've been in a state of . . . what do they call it . . . suspended animation. I haven't been able to plan anything. Haven't been able to work. Hardly been able to go out. Everybody I meet, either they want to avoid me or they want to talk about the blessed case. I mean suppose I had seen you? Then what would we have talked about, eh?
Lynne We needn't have talked at all.
Jack I'll tell you what we'd have talked about—we'd have talked about the case, right? Because that's been it. For six months that's been it.
Lynne Well, yeah, I can understand that.
Jack I haven't been able to think about the future. Because until that verdict today I didn't have a future. It's been weird.
Lynne And how's Maggie taken it?
Jack Oh, she's been wonderful. Stood by me all the way.
Lynne I'm glad.
Jack I suppose if there's any good come out of it, that's been it. Me and Maggie.
Lynne Only last time I talked to you, things were apparently getting a bit rocky, weren't they?

He looks at her in apparent surprise

Before everything happened. You said you didn't even know whether you'd be staying together.
Jack I don't remember saying anything like that.
Lynne You don't?
Jack No.
Lynne Well, all right, don't let's fall out about it. Hey, and I do like Maggie, don't get me wrong. She's a lovely girl.
Jack She is.

A pause

Lynne So then.
Jack What?
Lynne Are we going to try and resuscitate this tired, old affair of ours?
Jack Keep your voice down.
Lynne I don't mean now. Unless you fancy popping out into the garden for
a quick ... ?

Jack says nothing. He goes to pour himself another drink

No, well, some time more convenient then?

Still he says nothing

Or don't you think it will resuscitate? You think it's had it, is that it, Jack?
Because I'd rather you came straight out and said it. I don't want to have
to spend every night gazing at your bedroom window and playing Everley
Brothers records. I'm a bit long in the tooth for all that broken-hearted
teenage stuff.
Jack Lynne, I've had one hell of a day.
Lynne You've said.
Jack I've been in court. I've been acquitted of manslaughter. I've been out
celebrating. I've been pestered by reporters and photographers.
Lynne And now me.
Jack I'm just saying this isn't the best moment for some big, emotional,
cards-on-the-table session. I mean let's just, you know, let's just cool it for
a while.
Lynne Cool it? Cool it?
Jack Quiet!
Lynne You couldn't get any more cool than you've been towards me for the
last six months. And, all right, you've been preoccupied. You've had
things on your mind. Well, everybody has things on their mind, Jack. I
sometimes have so many things on my mind I don't think I'm going to
have any mind left!
Jack Look, I'm still very fond of you.
Lynne Or, to put it another way—get lost.
Jack I haven't said that.
Lynne You don't have to. I can do the translation for myself.
Jack Oh, come on ...

But, to his alarm, she moves to the kitchen door and opens it

Hey, what are you——
Lynne (*calling*) Maggie?
Maggie (*off*) Yes?
Jack Lynne ...
Lynne Do you want a hand in there?
Maggie (*off*) No, I'm all right, thanks.
Lynne OK then. (*She returns to Jack; with a barbed smile*) Oh, don't worry.
I do know the rules.

Jack I'm sure you do.

Lynne Which is why you put up with me for so long I suppose.

Jack Hey, come on. What's with all the hostility?

Lynne Oh, am I not doing it properly? You want us to shake hands and wish one another all the best in the future . . . ?

Jack Listen, I'll tell you something.

As Lynne helps herself to another drink

Yeah, help yourself.

Lynne I will.

Jack One thing I've realized—I want to marry Maggie. I want to have kids. And so I don't want anything else in my life that might, you know, jeopardize that.

Lynne Like me.

Jack Like any other relationship.

Lynne Well. Do have a lot to celebrate tonight, don't we.

We hear the front door, and Dennis enters

Jack Ah. Supplies have got through.

Dennis (*giving her the cigarettes*) You all right?

Lynne Yeah. Course I am.

Dennis (*to Jack*) Listen, this is probably no cause for alarm . . . Well, when I was out there, I noticed a car. Parked, what, fifty or sixty yards down the road. Why I noticed it was because there were these two men sitting in it. So when I was coming back I had another look. They're still there.

Maggie enters, with sandwiches

Maggie I did two rounds of salmon and one of cheese. So fight over 'em yourselves because my stomach is definitely not interested. (*She looks from Jack to Dennis*) What's the matter?

Jack Nothing, nothing. Just, er . . . talk among yourselves for two minutes, OK.

Jack goes out to the kitchen

Maggie Oh, well, anyway, there they are for anybody that wants 'em.

Dennis You know those characters you were telling us about—that did the shouting at the end of the trial . . . ?

Maggie Yes?

Dennis What did they look like?

Maggie Look like?

Dennis Hmm.

Maggie Well, they were . . . there was a woman and two men. One was older. I took him to be the dead man's father. And the other was perhaps his brother, I don't know. But why?

Dennis (*dismissively*) Oh . . .

Lynne They're out there in a car.

Maggie (*alarmed*) No . . . !

Dennis They might be. Only might be. We don't know it's them.

Maggie But there are three ... ?

Dennis No, two. Two men. But they could be anybody.

Maggie And what're they doing?

Dennis Just, you know, sitting there.

Maggie Watching the house?

Dennis Well, they're facing this way. I mean the car's facing this way.

Maggie Well, it must be them. Who else would it be out there at this time of night?

Jack returns, carrying a shotgun

This prompts expressions of alarm from the others

Dennis Oh, Christ.

Maggie Jack ... ?

Jack It's all right. I just fancy a little walk.

Maggie No, please! No, you're not going out. Not with that!

Jack Some people walk their dogs. I'm walking this.

Maggie And you're going to shoot somebody, is that the idea?

Jack No. Just want to make sure they aren't out to shoot me.

Maggie I'm going to call the police.

Jack OK, but all they'll do is come and arrest me for carrying this thing. That's all the police are going to do. Now, if that's what you want—go ahead and ring. Me, I'm just out for a quiet stroll. Shan't be long.

Jack goes out R

Maggie Dennis, stop him!

Dennis Me? When have you ever known him listen to me? (*During the next, he goes to the curtained french windows and looks out*)

Maggie Well, then I am going to ring the police. (*But she hesitates*) Lynne, you think I should, don't you?

Lynne Up to you, love.

Maggie But somebody's going to get killed!

Lynne I suppose it's possible.

Dennis (*looking out of the french windows*) Can you turn the main lights off?

Maggie What?

Dennis I can't see.

Lynne switches the main lights off

Ah. Yes.

Maggie What's happening? (*She goes to join him at the window*)

Dennis He's at the gate.

Maggie Oh no. (*She leaves the window, moves towards the door*) I'm going to go out.

Lynne I wouldn't if I were you.

Dennis He's going towards the car.

A moment as they all wait. Then we hear a distant engine start

Ah.

Maggie What?

The car moves away

Dennis It's all right. They're going.

Maggie Yes?

Dennis (*leaving the window*) Car's driven off.

Maggie Thank God.

Lynne So Jack wins again.

Dennis Yup. The man in the white, broad-brimmed stetson lives to fight another day.

Lynne It took guts though, going out like that.

Dennis Or the willingness to blow out somebody else's.

Lynne And you'd have done it, would you?

Dennis Probably not.

Maggie switches the light on again

Jack enters with the gun

Maggie Oh, Jack ...

Jack Hiya, kid. (*And gives her a kiss*) Just what I needed, that. Stroll in the night air.

Maggie What did they do? Did they say anything?

Jack Who? Oh, the two gents in the car? No, didn't say a dickie-bird. Just drove off.

Lynne I'm not surprised, seeing you waving your great blunderbuss at 'em.

Jack I beg your pardon?

Lynne gives a tight smile

Maggie Did you get the number of the car?

Jack No.

Maggie We could have checked it with the police. Found out if it really was them.

Jack But why? They've gone. Skidoodled. If they wanted me, I was there. But no, they were off like frightened rabbits.

Lynne That's if it was them.

Jack Well, if it wasn't, then I've just scared the shit out of a couple of courting insomniacs.

Maggie Jack, can you take that gun out of here, please.

Jack Don't worry. I'm not going to shoot anybody. I mean I've done that once, haven't I. And look at all the trouble that got me into.

He goes out to the kitchen

Maggie Might they come back, do you think?

Lynne I doubt it after that reception.

Maggie I still think we ought to ring the police. Let them know what's happened.

Lynne You never know, that might have been the police. In which case I shouldn't think it'll be long before they're ringing you.

Maggie They didn't look like policemen, did they, Dennis?

Dennis shakes his head

Jack returns

Jack Ah, sandwiches. Nothing like a bit of fresh air for putting an edge on your appetite. (*He starts to eat*)

Maggie Jack, I think we should ring the police and tell them what's happened.

Jack Nothing happened. Save I took out my blunderbuss in public, and they wouldn't like that.

Maggie But at least they could, you know, go to these people and warn them to stay away from here.

Jack I should think I've already done that. In a rather more persuasive fashion than the police would ever manage.

Dennis Where do they live?

They look at him

This family? Not round here, is it?

Lynne Why? What does it matter?

Dennis I just have the feeling I've read it somewhere.

Jack Fairfields.

Dennis Ah.

Jack Not the most salubrious area of this fair city. In fact, a festering cess-pit would have a lot more to recommend it. And I should think they're well on their way back there by now. By the way, Dennis, I do have a licence for that shotgun. In case you were wondering.

Dennis I wasn't, no.

Jack Don't want to be breaking the law, do we. And, Maggie, my sweet, I know you're still worried and you want to ring the police and all that . . .

Maggie I don't see what harm it can do.

Jack And I don't see what good it can do. So what if they park a panda car outside that front gate for a couple of hours? It's like I said. The state can't protect each and every one of us, and we've got to accept that. We're adults. We've got to take responsibility. Is nobody else eating these sandwiches?

Lynne You seem to be doing all right on your own.

Jack Well, have a drink then. Come on, it's supposed to be a party, is this. (*He helps himself to a drink*)

　　　　　　　For there's a guard and there's a sad old padre.
　　　　　　　And on and on we'll walk at daybreak.
　　　　　　　And then I'll touch the green, green grass . . .

Hey, but you should have seen their faces. They couldn't believe what they were seeing.

Maggie I'm sure they couldn't.

Jack And talk about a quick getaway. Vroom. Bat out of hell time.

Dennis I once ended up in Fairfields.

They look at him

Fairfields. Where they . . .

Lynne Did you.

Dennis Yes.

Jack And you survived to tell the tale, eh. Aren't many do that.

Dennis No. Mind, I wasn't intending to go there. I was intending to go and see *Casablanca*.

Jack Well, you came badly unstuck if you ended up seeing Fairfields instead of Casablanca. Badly unstuck.

Dennis It was the College film society. We show films every second Wednesday, you see. During term-time.

Lynne Dennis, what are you going on about?

Dennis I'm explaining how I came to be in Fairfields when, in point of fact, I had set out to see the film *Casablanca*.

Lynne But we'll take your word for it. I mean I'm sure nobody's all that interested.

Maggie peers out through the curtains

Jack And just what are you expecting to see out there?

Maggie I'm hoping I won't see anything.

Jack Give it half an hour and I'll go and have another look round.

Maggie No!

Jack Yes. Now calm down. Have a drink. Relax.

Dennis The film hadn't arrived, you see.

Lynne Oh, for goodness' sake ... !

Jack What film's that, Dennis?

Dennis *Casablanca*.

Jack Oh, right.

Dennis Hadn't arrived.

Jack No, well ... shame.

Lynne It is.

Dennis It hadn't been sent on promptly by the people who'd had it before us. Sometimes happens. So, anyway, I left the College and drove into the city centre. I thought I'd see what the regular cinemas were showing. But whatever it was—I can't remember now—whatever it was, I didn't fancy it.

Lynne Dennis.

Dennis What?

Lynne Why're you telling us all this?

Dennis I'm explaining how I came to be in Fairfields.

Lynne Well, it's all right. We don't want to know.

Jack I do. I want to know.

Lynne Oh, well, you listen to him then.

Dennis So, like I say, I'd drawn a blank all round as far as films were concerned.

Jack Yes.

Dennis So I thought what should I do? Because I didn't fancy going home either.

Jack No?

Dennis Lynne was working so the house would be empty.

Jack I see.

Dennis So I thought, well, I'll just cruise around. Have a drive round. Listen to the radio. I mean sometimes that's all you want to do, isn't it. Just keep on driving, heading for nowhere special.

Lynne I think that's what we're doing now—heading for nowhere special.

Jack Leave him alone. He's enjoying himself. Go on, Dennis. What happened next?

Dennis Well, I found myself over the other side of the city, over in Ryelands. You know Ryelands . . . ?

Jack Yes, we all know Ryelands, don't we?

Maggie Yes.

Jack Lynne, you know Ryelands?

Lynne Yeah.

Jack We're with you, Dennis. Go on.

Dennis Well, I was in that area. And it occured to me I might take the opportunity to call on an ex-colleague of mine. He left teaching to sell encyclopaedias. I thought I'd find out how he was going on.

Jack And how was he going on?

Dennis Well, no, I never found out. I mean I found his house all right, but it turned out there was nobody at home.

Jack Ah. Well, perhaps he was out on his rounds, you know selling the old encyclopaedias.

Dennis Yes, I thought that.

Lynne Or perhaps he was out because he saw you coming and didn't want to waste his time having to listen to all this.

Maggie (*amused*) I'm getting quite interested.

Jack Oh, I'm fascinated. So let's see if we've got this right, Dennis. *Casablanca*'s a dead loss, there's nothing else you fancy seeing and your mate's not home.

Dennis Yes.

Jack Right go on.

Dennis Well, it started to rain.

Amused reactions

Jack We should have guessed.

Dennis So I went back to the car.

Maggie But it wouldn't start.

Jack Or it had been nicked. One or the other.

Dennis No, no, it was still there. And it started all right.

Jack Things are looking up.

Lynne I'm becoming embarrassed by this, I really am.

Jack No, don't be embarrassed.

Maggie It's a better story than *Casablanca*.

Lynne Do you think. (*To Dennis*) Right, so have you finished? Is that it?

Dennis So I got back to the car . . .

Lynne groans. Jack and Maggie are amused

And I decided I should go home after all.

Lynne I think we both should.

Dennis What I also decided was that I'd drive straight across the city centre. Rather than take the ring road. Because it was evening, you see. Not much traffic.

Jack Good thinking.

Dennis But then . . .

Jack Oh-oh.

Maggie More problems?

Dennis Well, yes, I came to a set of road works.

Jack Course you did.

Dennis With diversion signs taking me off the road I was following. So I obeyed the diversion signs till all of a sudden they just stopped appearing. Leaving me not knowing where I was.

Lynne We haven't known where you've been since you started.

Dennis And then I drove around a bit further. Saw a few road signs. And that's when I realized I was in Fairfields.

Jack Ah . . . !

Maggie All is now revealed.

Lynne Well, thank goodness for that.

Dennis I suppose I must have passed it before but I'd never, you know, viewed it from the inside. All high-rise flats, maisonettes, that sort of thing.

Jack Like Alcatraz, but without the sea views.

Dennis And just as difficult to get out of. I seemed to be driving round and round in ever decreasing circles. Then I came across a pub. Which looked pretty horrendous, I must admit. But by then I was past caring. So I stopped and went in for a drink.

Jack I think you deserved one.

Maggie By the way, there are still some sandwiches left, if anybody wants.

Lynne Yes, I will. Bugger the diet. Anyway, the one I'm on does allow you one blow-out every month.

Maggie Oh, well, you're all right then.

Lynne Not really. I've already used up my allocation for the next five years.

Jack Ladies, ladies. I suspect Dennis hasn't quite come to the end of this amazing tale.

Lynne Will he ever.

Dennis I haven't quite, no. See, once I was in the pub, I found there was somebody there I knew.

Jack Not Humphrey Bogart . . . ? (*He imitates*) "Out of all the pubs in all the world . . ."

Dennis No.

Jack Oh. Well, just a thought.

Dennis It was a young man, somebody I'd once taught.

Jack I see.

Lynne And is that it. End of story, is it?

Dennis He'd been on a day-release course when I'd taught him. Doing his City and Guilds.

Lynne It's not, is it. He's going to go on forever.

Maggie I think he is.

Dennis To be honest, I didn't remember him at first. But evidently he remembered me.

Lynne Well, yes, he would.

Dennis So we got talking. Apparently he'd jacked in the City and Guilds. Jacked in most things by the sound of it. It was a funny conversation. One of those where you meet somebody you don't really know, have a drink or two, and suddenly you're telling one another all sorts of intimate secrets that you can only tell to someone you think you'll never see again.

Jack Oh, yeah? And what sort of secrets were these then, Dennis?

Maggie Well, we aren't strangers, are we. Perhaps Dennis would rather not tell us.

Jack Only joking. No, don't tell us if you don't want to.

Dennis He was unemployed, this young man. Had been for three years.

Lynne He does want to.

Dennis He said he was desperate for money. Said he'd do anything for it. I said like what? He said anything. Kill for it if he had to.

Jack Sounds like just the sort of entrepreneur this government's trying to promote.

Dennis Well, yes.

Jack So what did you say?

Dennis I asked him what sort of things he'd tried. And he told me. Burglary mostly. Breaking-and-entering. In fact, he'd been caught and spent six months in prison.

A pause

Lynne Are you making this up?

Dennis No.

Jack And what was his name, this enterprising youth?

Dennis I'm coming to that. So I said well, did that mean he'd given up burglary then? He said more or less, yes. He said he'd thought about becoming a hit-man, a contract killer. Which at first I took as a joke. Admittedly I didn't know Fairfields, but it seemed an unlikely centre for contract killers, even apprentice ones.

Jack What was his name?

Dennis (*ignoring Jack*) I said surely he couldn't really mean that if somebody paid him then he'd go out and kill—in cold blood—kill somebody he didn't even know . . . ? But he said yes, he would. And I said well then, he had a choice. Either he joined the Italian Mafia or the British SAS . . .

No reaction

No, he didn't laugh either.

Jack His name, for Christ's sake?

Dennis (*still not answering Jack*) So then he asked me—how was I? What had been happening in my life? And, because he'd told me so much about himself, or anyway seemed to have, I answered in a fairly forthright fashion. Told him I was still working at the College and . . . and that I was feeling pretty desperate too—in my own way. I was desperate because I felt I was losing my wife to another man and didn't know what to do about it.

A pause

Lynne I hope you know what you're saying.

Dennis Oh yes, yes. It's a relief to be able to say it actually. Since I've thought about little else for God knows how long.

Maggie I don't think we should be hearing this.

Jack Oh, I'm sure Dennis hasn't finished yet. Have you, Dennis?

Dennis And I said to him, how much would he charge me to kill this man? I mean assuming he was serious about what he'd said earlier. And he said yes, he was serious and that he'd charge me ten thousand pounds.

Maggie Is it some kind of joke?

Lynne Sick joke.

Jack And you said?

Dennis Well, I must have looked rather taken aback at the ten thousand because he said OK then, eight. Eight thousand. So I said you're on. And we shook hands on it.

Jack Sounds like you got a bargain.

Maggie Look, if it is a joke, I don't think it's a very funny one.

Lynne I'm not exactly rolling about either.

Dennis Anyway, that was where we left it, that particular night. We agreed to meet again two weeks later. You see, that would be the next film society meeting.

Jack And what were they showing?

Dennis *The Maltese Falcon.*

Jack Good film.

Dennis Yes, well, I'd seen it before. So I gave it a miss this time and went back to that pub instead. Oddly enough, I drove straight to it without any problem.

Jack Well, I think we're all pleased to hear that.

Dennis I really didn't think he'd be there. But he was, standing at the bar like before. Course he hadn't expected me to turn up either, so we both had to start again convincing one another we were both serious. Did I still want this man killing? I said yes. Was he still willing to do it? And he said yes, he was. So I gave him four thousand pounds. Cash of course. And promised to pay him the other four, the balance, when the job was done.

Lynne You're out of your mind, you know that?

Maggie Jack . . .

Jack Wait.

Lynne I said you're out of your mind! For one thing where would you get four thousand pounds without me knowing?

Dennis I borrowed it.

Lynne Where from?

Dennis Finance company.

Lynne stares. She has no reply

Of course I had to give him the name of the victim. His address. Details like that.

Lynne Yes, well, we don't want to hear 'em, Dennis, we don't!

Dennis And we agreed that we'd meet again, in that same pub, the night after the job was done. So that I could hand over the other four thousand. Only, of course, we never did because . . . well, things didn't work out.

Jack Did they not.

Dennis No.

Jack You mean—because I killed him before he could kill me?

A pause

Dennis Yes.

Maggie No.

Lynne We're going. We are going now, this minute.

Dennis And his name was Philip Mercer, as if you didn't already know. And I paid him to kill you because of what you've done to my marriage!

Jack Well, then perhaps you should get your money back. Because he didn't do a very good job, did he.

Dennis At least now you know. You know the real reason he came here!

Jack I know you're off your head, that's all I know.

Lynne Can we please just go?

Dennis I've seen her watching, just waiting to see you leaving the house.

Jack I think Lynne's anxious you should go.

Dennis And sometimes . . . sometimes when she's been on what she calls her girls' night out, I've been able to smell you on her when she's come back.

Jack Now *I'm* getting anxious you should go.

Dennis And he might have failed. Philip Mercer might have failed to kill you. And I have his death on my conscience because I'm the one that sent him to it. But I swear here and now if you so much as look at my wife again I'll come looking for you and I'll do the job myself next time. Come on.

Dennis goes. Lynne follows him. There is a pause as they go

Jack Hmm. Does get himself worked up sometimes, does Dennis. Probably all these films. Get him over-excited.

Maggie Jack, don't treat me like an imbecile, please.

Jack What?

Maggie I want the truth. Will you just tell me the truth, please.

Jack Certainly. I've been telling it all day, under oath some of it. I'm getting to be quite an expert.

Maggie About you and Lynne. All that that Dennis was saying.

Jack Dennis is crazy. And crazy people shouldn't be taken too much notice of. Best to let 'em rant on. Then eventually they get tired and fall asleep.

Maggie Have you been having an affair with Lynne? Yes or no?

Jack Yes. Well . . . no . . . Not recently.

Maggie Thank you.

Jack We did have—what would you call it?—an understanding. But it's all over. Finished. Ancient history.

Maggie Dennis doesn't think so.

Jack Dennis needs psychiatric help. And the psychiatrist that gives it him, he'll probably need it as well.

Maggie You and Lynne . . . you were lovers, yes?

Jack Lovers? Oh . . . (*He grimaces*) We sometimes went to bed together. But it wasn't any great romance. Not even great sex. It was just something we did occasionally. So don't let it come between us, Maggie. Don't. It's not worth that. Never was. I mean, if you want to know then . . . well, I was lonely. Suzanne had left and . . . I was lonely. And Lynne was . . . (*He hesitates*)

Maggie Lonely.

Jack Available.

Maggie Ha. And what about the rest of Dennis' story?

Jack What, this convoluted tale about going to Fairfields and bumping into a budding hit-man . . . ?

Maggie Yes.

Jack No way.

Maggie You don't believe him?

Jack Dennis is the last of the great, white liberals. He couldn't plan a murder to save his life.

Maggie But if he hated you enough, Jack . . .

Jack Then he'd go to a solicitor. Or get up a petition, or put forward a motion to be debated at the next film society wine-and-cheese party. What he would not do is go scouring bars, looking for cut-rate mercenaries.

Maggie He believed you were threatening his marriage.

Jack I wasn't.

Maggie But if he believed it . . .

Jack Maggie, Dennis is one of life's idealists, one of life's dreamers, one of life's wankers.

Maggie He loves Lynne and he thought you were trying to take her away from him.

Jack So why didn't he say anything to her about it?

Maggie Because he was frightened of what might happen if he did. That she might leave him. He doesn't know that as far as you're concerned it's just casual, just sex, does he?

Jack Hey, hey, come on.

Maggie Well, you're being very stupid, Jack.

Jack Be on my side. Please. I've had enough people out to kill me for one day.

Maggie I'm not out to kill you.

Jack Then marry me.

Maggie (*ignoring that*) I mean for one thing . . .

Jack What?

Maggie Something I never understood all the way through the trial. The man who broke in here, Philip Mercer, what was he doing carrying a gun in the first place?

Jack Why not? He's a criminal.

Maggie A burglar. But he wasn't carrying anything else, was he. No tools or anything. Just a gun.

Jack So he wasn't a very good burglar.

Maggie reacts dismissively

Well, how the hell should I know? Maybe he lost his tools. Maybe he had
'em stolen. But one thing I do know—Dennis didn't send him.

Maggie So why should he claim he did?

Jack Because—because, well, all right, maybe he does think I'm liable to
run off with his wife. Which is bullshit. But maybe he's got it into his head
and it's festering away and so he comes up with this fantasy. But that's all
it is. Fantasy. I mean for one thing why tell us now? Tonight of all nights?
Why keep quiet for six months, then give us the full, unexpurgated load of
crap tonight?

Maggie Because he was expecting you'd be found guilty.

Jack Hoping I would be.

Maggie Possibly.

Jack Definitely. He was rooting for it along with Judge Jeffreys and the
rest. He's not a Mason, is he, Dennis? Only, if he cared to apply, I'm sure
they'd look on him very favourably.

Maggie He was expecting you to be found guilty. Then found you weren't.
You were still going to be here, still living next-door. So the only thing left
to him is to tell you the truth about Philip Mercer. Hoping that that, if
nothing else, will keep you away from Lynne.

Jack He doesn't have to keep me away from Lynne.

Maggie He thinks he does. Why else should Philip Mercer be carrying a
gun? Can't you see how it makes sense of everything?

Jack No.

Maggie Because you don't want to see it. In case I start wondering just how
involved you and Lynne really were. I mean I might decide not to accept
this take-it-or-leave-it line you're trying to sell me.

Jack I wasn't involved.

Maggie You used to sleep with her.

Jack Sometimes.

Maggie Enough times for her husband to pay somebody to kill you!

Jack You know what I don't understand. Earlier today twelve perfect
strangers listened to me and and they believed me. Now you—not a
stranger—in fact, the one person I want to spend the rest of my life with—
you don't believe me.

Maggie Because I can't believe that Dennis was lying.

A pause

Jack All right.

Maggie What?

Jack You want me to prove it?

Maggie Prove ... ?

Jack Prove he was lying.

Maggie How?

Jack By telling you what really happened.

Maggie What really happened . . . ?

Jack nods

You mean it wasn't what Dennis said?
Jack No.
Maggie And it wasn't what you said in court?
Jack No.

A pause

Maggie Tell me.

Black-out

CURTAIN

ACT II

The same. Immediately following

The action is continuous from the end of Act I. Thus, Maggie is still waiting for Jack's explanation

Maggie (*repeating*) Tell me.

Jack I'm going to. But let the record show it's under protest, right? I'm only telling you so you'll know that poor, crazy Dennis was talking through his backside.

Maggie I don't care *why*, Jack. I want you to tell me what happened.

Jack All right, all right. Then cast your mind back, as they say. Six months ago. Jan. twenty-first. You remember?

Maggie Yes.

Jack It hadn't exactly been the greatest night of my life. Even before I shot Philip Mercer.

Maggie No.

Jack You were hell-bent on leaving. Packing your bags and departing for pastures new. Or old. But anyway pastures different. Whereas I wasn't too keen on the idea and so we discussed the matter.

Maggie Ha.

Jack Well, yeah. More fight than discussion, yes?

Maggie Yes.

Jack Championship bout.

Maggie We slugged it out.

Jack Slugged it out. Blood everywhere. Fifteen rounder. With me on the canvas.

Maggie Me too.

Jack Well, but you were still leaving. I hadn't managed to change your mind. Oh, and you remember what caused all this? What put the idea of leaving into your head in the first place?

Maggie (*looking at him; then*) Meeting Suzanne ...?

Jack Right.

Maggie That wasn't what put the idea into my head.

Jack You'd bumped into good old Suzanne. My ex-wife. Ex-wife number two to give her full title. You'd met her ... where was it you'd met her?

Maggie At the bank. But that wasn't——

Jack At the bank. Both of you there, cashing cheques. Always good at that was Sue. Left a trail of cheques behind her wherever she went. As if she was afraid she might get lost and have to use 'em to find her way home again.

Maggie Jack, please.

Jack What?

Maggie Can you just tell me what happened? I mean without all this raking over . . .

Jack I'm doing it. I'm doing it. This is all relevant. Just trust me.

Maggie Go on.

Jack Earlier that day you'd met Sue in a bank. (*He mimics*) "Oh, hallo, aren't you . . . ?" "Well, yes, and you must be . . ." Et cetera, et cetera. And you end up having coffee together. Sharing experiences. Exchanging impressions of Life With Jack. Which I can understand. I mean what else are you going to talk about? What else do you have in common? My ex-wife and the lady I'm living with. You're not going to start swapping recipes.

Maggie Jack, do you want us to have that row all over again? Is that what you're working up to?

Jack No.

Maggie You want me to tell you all over again that I want to go?

Jack No! Last thing. I want you to tell me you'll marry me, that's what I want you to tell me.

Maggie Go on.

Jack Only I need to remind you what it was like. The atmosphere between us. Everything.

Maggie I know what it was like.

Jack You'd talked to Suzanne and she's fed you this picture of me as some kind of monster. Bluebeard. Fee-fi-fo-fum, I smell the blood . . . all that. And she told you you had to escape. Get back down the beanstalk, little girl, while you have the chance.

Maggie I'll tell you one thing she did say, shall I?

Jack What?

Maggie She said you patronize women.

Jack Patronize . . . ?

Maggie Like you're doing now. Exactly like you're doing now.

Jack I don't patronize. Subsidize! That's what I do—I subsidize women.

Maggie stands

What? What're you doing?

Maggie I'm going to bed.

Jack No, no, Maggie please. I'm trying to tell you what happened. You might not think so but I am. Sit down. Please sit down. Let me get you a drink. What would you like?

Maggie Nothing.

Jack But sit down. Please.

Maggie does

Now I know you don't want it but I'll get you a brandy. So it's there in case you change your mind. Or for something to throw at me. You never know when you might need that. And you know I love you, right? You know that?

Maggie Yes.

Jack Good. So, whatever we say, whatever flak happens to be flying, it's basically because I love (*he kisses her*) you.

Maggie Did you love Suzanne?

Jack Did I . . . ?

Maggie Love Suzanne? And Janice or whatever your first wife was called. Did you love her?

Jack I suppose . . . must have. But then I used to wear flared trousers, I can't understand why I did that either. Come on, what is this?

Maggie I just wondered.

Jack You wondering what I did to drive them both away?

Maggie says nothing

Well, I'll let you into a secret. So am I. I've been wondering about that for a long time. But it won't happen again. Not with you. Never.

Maggie Please tell me if you're going to.

Jack What happened?

Maggie Yes.

Jack Right. To the point. No more pissing about. The scene is set. We'd had a fight. A bruising encounter. Which, just for the record again, had followed you and Suzanne meeting at the bank. Then you'd come home, announced you were leaving. I didn't want you to. But you're not listening. You're still leaving. Only not straightaway. It was late. You were tired. Have I missed anything out?

Maggie No.

Jack Good. So you went to bed. Bed in the spare room. First, small step of your intended departure. Which leaves me down here, trying to make sense of it all and not managing to. Then I hear noises from out there. Somebody breaking in. As if I don't have enough on my plate with the woman I love telling me she's off first thing in the morning, some yobbo is trying to kick his way through my back door. Fortunately he doesn't find it very easy. Takes him a minute or two. Which gives me time to go out into that hallway and collect the gun I have tucked away in the cabinet out there.

Maggie (*taken aback*) The gun *you* have . . . ?

Jack Yeah.

Maggie It was yours?

Jack Yeah.

Maggie Not . . .

Jack Not Philip Mercer's, no. It was mine. Exhibit B. Smith-and-Wesson four-point-four. Which was why I knew all along that Dennis's story was just wishful thinking. Fantasy.

A pause

Maggie Did Philip Mercer have a gun with him when he came in here?

Jack No.

Maggie So the only gun . . .

Jack Was mine.

Maggie And everything you said in court . . .

Jack Was a lie. Yes, sorry about that. Sometimes you just have these things to do. I mean self-preservation, it's a powerful instinct.

Maggie If it was your gun, then why haven't I ever seen it?

Jack Because you didn't know where to look.

Maggie You said it was in the cabinet . . .

Jack Hidden. You wouldn't find it unless you knew about it. There's like a secret drawer, secret compartment in the side. Show you if you like.

Maggie And where did you get it, the gun?

Jack Honestly can't remember. They come my way occasionally. Usually when somebody's inherited a load of old junk and they want rid. Turn out the attics and lofts of this country and you could equip an army. (*He pauses*) It was my gun, Maggie. All that that Dennis said . . . load of bullshit. He didn't recruit Philip Mercer or anybody else to kill me. He probably went to see his film, fell asleep and dreamt it.

Maggie Philip Mercer really was just a burglar.

Jack You've got it.

Maggie Unarmed.

Jack Unarmed.

Maggie So what happened when he came in here?

Jack Well, like I say, he took a minute or two to break in. I've got the gun and I've come back in here, and I'm standing about here, waiting for him. Oh, I'd switched the light off. So all I can see is that door opening. And then a shape. So I switch the light back on. And he's standing there, staring at me. And then I, er . . . shot him.

Maggie What, you just . . .

Jack Shot him, yes. Bang.

Maggie No.

Jack 'Fraid so.

Maggie But why?

Jack Criminal, wasn't he. Making war on society. Well, society hit back for once.

Maggie But there must have been . . . I mean wasn't there any kind of struggle or . . .

Jack No. He stood there. I stood there. Bang.

Maggie That's murder.

Jack Well technically I suppose . . .

Maggie Jack, that's murder. What you've said is murder!

Jack If you say so. I'm not too clued up on the legal side.

Maggie Why couldn't you have just kept him here? Kept him and rung for the police? Why did you have to shoot him?

Jack Why?

Maggie Yes, why?

Jack To stop you leaving.

A pause

Maggie I don't . . .

Jack Like you were planning to. You'd gone to bed saying you were going to leave next morning. You were set on it. Well, in those few seconds before he got in here, while I was standing here with the gun, I had this sort of vision. Vision of the future. All of a sudden I could see everything, how it could happen. Me killing him, police arriving, interviews . . . even the manslaughter charge. Then me in court and the trial. I saw it all, every step of the way. Only thing I couldn't see was the verdict, but I had to take a chance on that. And do you know what I could see most clearly?

Maggie shakes her head

Most clearly I could see how it would stop you leaving. With all that going on, the trial hanging over me . . . well, you wouldn't be able to go, would you. You'd have to stick by me. See it through. Which you did.

A pause

Maggie No.
Jack Yes.
Maggie You can't have killed a man just for that!
Jack You wanted the truth. I warned you you might not like it.
Maggie It's murder, Jack. A young man like that, you murdered him . . . ! In cold blood! I mean Christ, Jack, how could you? A cold-blooded murder!
Jack There was nothing cold-blooded about it. We're talking middle of the night, somebody breaking in. I'm standing here, wetting myself, wondering what's going to come through that door!
Maggie You still didn't have to . . .
Jack And let's not forget something else either. He was a common criminal, right? Out to ransack my house. Everything that was said at the trial, all that is still true. I was protecting my house and my property. As I was justified in doing.
Maggie He was a young man . . .
Jack So? That doesn't make him a boy scout. Breaking in here as part of some Outward Bound course. He was a criminal. Engaged in criminal activity.
Maggie So that gives you *carte blanche* to shoot him, does it?
Jack (*after hesitation*) Yes.
Maggie God.
Jack As the jury agreed. Let's not forget that.
Maggie Because they didn't know the facts. They didn't know it was your gun.
Jack They knew enough. No point in confusing 'em.
Maggie And they certainly didn't know you shot him to stop me walking out on you.

A pause

Jack Look Maggie, I didn't enjoy shooting him. Don't start thinking of me as some kind of monster.
Maggie Fee-fi-fo-fum.
Jack And listen. Nobody else knows what happened. Just me and you. And we don't ever have to refer to it again. Not even between the two of us.

Let's go back to the authorized version. The one that was spelled out in court, the one that's going to be in the newspapers. It was his gun and I wrestled it from him.

No response

Yes?

Maggie So easy. Just forget all about it.

Jack Not easy, no. But what do you want? You want I should go out and confess? Ring that reporter, give him the story of a lifetime? Is that what you want?

Maggie (*after hesitating*) No.

Jack No, right, course you don't. Be two fingers up to all those nice people on the jury who found me not guilty, wouldn't it. I mean what sort of gratitude would that be? And then again, what could anybody do? I've been tried and found not guilty. They couldn't try me again. Did you know that?

Maggie Yes.

Jack You can't be tried twice for the same thing.

Maggie Yes.

A pause

Jack Look. I know you're upset. Course you are. I never intended to tell you any of this. Never would have if it hadn't been for crazy Dennis and his fantasies. But now it's over, so let's just put it behind us and think of the future, all right? I love you, Maggie. I want you to marry me.

The doorbell rings

Amazing. How do you do that?

Maggie Do what?

Jack Every time I mention marrying you, the doorbell rings. You've got it wired up or something? (*He moves to answer it*)

Maggie Jack, be careful.

Jack Of what?

Maggie Well, who can it be? At this time?

Jack (*looking at his watch*) Probably the milkman. Wanting to know whether we'll need an extra pint now I'm not going to be in prison.

Jack goes out to the hall. We hear the front door being opened

(*Off*) Ah.

Dennis (*off*) Can I have a word?

Jack (*off*) Yeah, come in. Party's still on. We're expecting a mobile disco any minute. RAF are flying in more booze as a humanitarian gesture.

He shows in Lynne and Dennis

Guests have returned. Couldn't keep away, they enjoyed it that much.

Lynne I'm sorry, love. But we thought it best to come back and get this sorted out.

Maggie nods

Jack Sit down.

But they don't. They stand together, perhaps hand-in-hand

Make yourselves at home. Let's freshen those drinks up. Oh, and look, we've still the odd sandwich left, not curling at the edges. No? Well, I will. It gives me an appetite, all this . . . fantasizing.

Dennis You, er . . . you know then?

Jack Know what? You tell me, Dennis.

Dennis It wasn't true.

Jack No?

Dennis What I said about me paying that young man and putting him up to coming here . . .

Jack Not true . . . ?

Dennis No.

Jack Well.

Dennis I got rather carried away.

Jack You can say that again.

Lynne For which he had good reason.

Dennis Anyway . . . there it is.

Lynne And something else you might like to know. As soon as we can arrange it, we're going to put our house up for sale.

Jack No . . . !

Lynne We're going to move. Somewhere away from here.

Jack Away from me.

Lynne Away from everything.

Jack Oh now, come on. Let's not, you know, get things out of proportion. Surely we can put all this behind us. Go back to being good neighbours . . . friends . . . I mean all right, build a high fence if you have to. Put up Keep Out signs. But don't move.

Lynne We've decided.

Jack Dennis, old pal . . .

Dennis Piss off.

Jack Suit yourself. But as my mother used to say—God bless her soul—she used to say, it'll all look different in the morning.

Lynne It's already the bloody morning, Jack. And yes, a lot of things do look different. Which is why it's best we move.

Jack Maggie, you tell 'em.

Maggie Tell them what?

Jack They mustn't move!

Maggie Perhaps they should.

Jack Huh. All that jury's fault, isn't it. All their fault. if they'd put me away, like they were supposed to, then you'd no doubt have been happy to stay. Eh, Dennis?

Dennis Probably.

Jack Definitely. I suppose I could appeal. Try and reverse the verdict. No, perhaps not. (*He looks at his watch*) Not just now anyway. 'Cause now, if you'll all excuse me, I'm just going to pop out for ten minutes.

Maggie Out?

Jack Yeah.

Maggie But why?

Jack Got to catch up on my reviews, haven't I. See what kind of write-ups I've got. Oh, but don't worry. I'm not walking this time. I'll take the car.

Maggie But where are you going to find newspapers at this time?

Jack Local distributor's a pal of mine. He reckons they arrive around now and I'm sure he won't begrudge me the odd copy. So, anyway, sorry I have to dash off. But do carry on. Be a shame to break up the party. Sandwiches. Drinks. Soon be breakfast if you want to hang on.

Maggie But why can't you wait?

Jack Because. I can't. Ten minutes.

Jack goes out

A pause

Dennis Remind me to cancel our papers. There are some stories I've already had more than a bellyful of.

Lynne Maggie, love . . . there was one other thing I wanted to say. Say to you.

Maggie Yes?

Lynne And that's I'm sorry you had to find out the way you did.

Dennis Oh well, my fault that . . .

Lynne Most of what happened was before Jack even knew you. After Suzanne had left him.

Maggie It's all right.

Lynne No, but I don't think it is, is it. I think it's upset you.

Maggie If anything's upset me, Lynne, it's nothing you've done.

Lynne Well, I'm sorry anyway. (*After a pause*) Right, well, we'll leave you to get some rest.

But before they can leave

Maggie Oh, no, don't go. I mean please wait, if you could just wait till Jack gets back . . .

Lynne (*doesn't mind*) Oh, well . . .

Maggie I just don't want to be left alone. It's pathetic, I know but . . .

Lynne No, we'll stay, love. Won't we?

Dennis Sure . . .

Maggie I shouldn't ask you, should I. I bet this is the last house in the world you want to be in.

Lynne Look, sit down and let me get you a drink. You look as though you need one.

Maggie I've got one. But you two help yourselves.

Dennis Not for me.

Lynne Well, I will then. Why not. I'm on to tomorrow's ration of calories now, aren't I. Dennis, love . . .

Dennis Go on.

Lynne Would you be an angel and go and get my fags for me?

Dennis Is that all you have to do to be an angel. Sounds easier than I thought.

Lynne Thanks.

Dennis exits

(*After a pause*) I do love Dennis, you know. It's just I tend to take him for granted. He's put up with a lot from me over the years. More than I'd ever put up with from him. (*After a pause*) I'll tell you something about Jack, shall I?

Maggie What?

Lynne He dotes on you. Absolutely dotes on you. He'd do anything for you.

Maggie Yes.

Lynne Absolutely anything.

Maggie I know.

Lynne Good. So perhaps we're all going to survive after all. Come out smiling. Cheers.

Maggie Cheers. (*Then*) You know when Dennis told that story ... ?

Lynne Story ... ?

Maggie About arranging to have Jack ...

Lynne Oh. That story, yeah.

Maggie How did you feel then?

Lynne How did I feel ... ?

Maggie Well, it was because of you, wasn't it. What he was saying was that he was willing to do that—to arrange a murder—in order to keep you.

Lynne I suppose—suppose he was.

Maggie What did it make you think about him?

Lynne Don't know really ...

Maggie You must do!

Lynne I didn't really have time ...

Maggie Did you feel proud of him? Or did it frighten you or ... what?

Lynne Maggie, I don't know what you're trying to get me to say.

Maggie (*giving up*) No.

Lynne And then I don't know that I ever really believed him. Not really.

A pause

Maggie Oh, God ... !

Lynne What?

Maggie shakes her head

Look you've had a long day. You've been under a lot of stress——

Maggie I've got to get out. I want to get away from here. In fact, I'm going to go now. I'm going to just clear out before he comes back!

Lynne Hey, come on ...

Maggie I have to!

Lynne Maggie, calm down, just calm down.

Maggie He wants to marry me.

Lynne Well ... so I gathered.

Maggie Well, I won't. I've got a life of my own. I don't care what he's done—he can't stop me leaving.

Lynne (*at a loss*) No.
Maggie But he will. I know he will. He controls me.
Lynne Perhaps you ... you know, need to get out more. Or get back to work. Used to be a designer, didn't you?
Maggie Yes. Well, no, that wasn't me. That was somebody else that used to be me. Now I'm Jack Lilley's girl-friend. That's the sum total of what my life's come to.
Lynne If you don't want to marry him ... well, then you must tell him.
Maggie I already have.
Lynne And what happened?

A moment. Maggie says nothing. The front door opens

Maggie Don't say anything to Dennis.
Lynne No.

Dennis comes in. He presents Lynne with her cigarettes and sits down

Oh, thanks love.
Dennis It's beginning to get light. Birds are singing.
Lynne So long as they don't expect us to join in.
Maggie Do you want a drink, Dennis, or ...
Dennis No, thank you. Nothing.

A pause

Lynne Sometimes when I'm on night duty and it gets to around this time, you'd swear there's a moment when you can actually feel it slipping from one day to the next. They say it's around then that most people die.
Maggie Philip James Mercer for example.
Lynne Well ... yes.

A pause

Dennis I did actually once meet him, you know. Philip Mercer.

They look at him in surprise

Oh, everything else ... didn't happen. I'm not trying to go back and say it did. But I did meet him. It was a while ago now. I bumped into him in that pub, the *Travellers*, the one we use from College.
Lynne You knew him then?
Dennis Yes. (*And quickly qualifies*) Well, knew him. I mean I once taught him. Probably only was once as well. He wasn't exactly one of our top attenders. Drop-out from the word go was Philip. I did tell you. When we first heard the name, I said I used to teach him.
Lynne Can't remember.
Dennis Though when you've taught thousands, I don't suppose it's any great coincidence. (*Then*) Now that was odd though.
Lynne What?
Dennis It's only just struck me.
Lynne What has?

Dennis He knew Jack.

Maggie Philip Mercer ... ?

Dennis (*nodding*) Knew Jack.

Lynne He couldn't have.

Dennis This time I'm talking about, when I bumped into him in the *Travellers*. Which was, what, nine months ago, perhaps a year. It was probably what gave me the idea for saying what I did say, come to think of it. But anyway ...

Lynne You met him in the *Travellers*.

Dennis Yeah. We were both at the bar. He said hallo, I bet you don't recognize me. Which I didn't really, though his face rang a bell. And then he told me who he was and I remembered teaching him. So we had the usual conversation. I asked him how he was going on, what he'd been doing. And he said what he'd been doing was six months in the nick for burglary. So I made a few sympathetic noises and bought him a beer.

Lynne You said he knew Jack.

Dennis Hang on a minute.

Lynne (*to Maggie*) He does ramble on.

Dennis He asked me what *I* was doing. And I said still teaching ... all that. And he asked me where I lived. I can't remember why ...

Lynne It doesn't matter why.

Dennis No. So, anyway, I told him, and that was when he said, oh, I know somebody else who lives down there. I said who. He said Jack Lilley. And then he said—he's a dealer, deals in antiques, secondhand jewellery, that sort of thing. And I said yeah, that's him.

Maggie Did he say how he knew him?

Dennis No. I think other people arrived. That was about all we said to one another.

Lynne So perhaps he didn't know Jack personally. Just knew who he was.

Dennis It didn't sound like that. He said he *knew* him.

Maggie But then why was it never mentioned? Not at the trial or before-hand or anytime?

Lynne He couldn't have known him.

Dennis He said he did.

Lynne Well, then he was ... I don't know what he was doing.

Maggie But you believed him ... ?

Dennis Philip Mercer ... ?

Maggie Yes.

Dennis Oh, yeah. No reason not to.

Maggie Then why was it never mentioned at the trial?

Dennis Well ... either because Jack never let on ...

Maggie (*in disbelief*) Never let on ... ?

Dennis Don't ask me why. But either he never let on. Or perhaps he did and ... well, perhaps it just never got raised at the trial because it never seemed relevant to what was at issue.

Maggie I don't believe that.

Dennis I don't believe that either.

Lynne It's not the only thing that wasn't mentioned at that trial.

They look at her

Maggie Why do you say that?
Lynne (*hesitating, then shaking her head*) No . . . no. Forget I said anything.
Dennis You haven't said anything.
Lynne It's something I should have said six months ago, and I didn't say it
   then so . . . (*She shakes her head again. Then*) Well, look, if I did tell you
   . . . well, it'd just have to be between us, all right?
Dennis Right.
Lynne I wouldn't want it going any further.
Maggie It won't.
Lynne (*hesitating, then shaking her head even more determinedly*) No . . . no,
   I can't.

They react

   Well, I'm sorry but it'd be wrong. If I didn't say it then, then it'd be wrong
   to say it now.
Dennis Is this something about Jack or the trial or what?
Maggie Or something about Philip Mercer?

Lynne shakes her head

Dennis Well, OK, nobody's going to force you.
Maggie Course they're not.
Lynne It's just I think there was somebody else in this house when Philip
   Mercer was killed. There.

A pause

Dennis Somebody else . . . ?
Maggie Well, there was me . . .
Lynne Besides you. Besides Jack. Another person.
Dennis Why? What's put that into your head?
Lynne I shouldn't have told you, should I. I shouldn't have said a word.
Dennis (*patiently*) Why do you think there was somebody else?
Lynne Because I saw him arrive. From our house, our lounge window. I
   was still up and I saw somebody arrive.
Dennis You're sure?
Lynne Yeah.
Maggie But who?
Lynne Well, it was a man. That's about all I could tell. He came to your
   front door, and Jack—I suppose it was Jack—let him in.
Dennis You've never said anything . . .
Lynne I know I've never said anything. I've told you that. And I'm not a bit
   sure I should be saying it now either.
Maggie But what time was this?
Lynne Oh, late. Well, I mean early morning. I'd been working a late shift,
   then I'd come home and I hadn't been able to settle. I always take a while
   to wind down. And, anyway, there's something about working with
   geriatrics that makes you want to stay awake for as long as you can. He

(*Dennis*) was snoring his head off. So I sat downstairs, reading a library book.

Dennis Had you been drinking?

Lynne And what's that supposed to mean?

Dennis Only asking.

Lynne Well, I might have had a glass of something-or-other. In fact I probably had. But nothing that'd stop me seeing straight.

Dennis No, OK, OK.

Lynne And what I did see—like I said—was somebody arrive and Jack let him in.

Dennis But why haven't you told this to anybody before? To the police?

Lynne Well, because . . . oh, I don't know. I mean first of all there was all the commotion . . . police-cars, ambulances . . . and I wasn't going to go rushing forward into that lot. And then I didn't know what'd happened, not really, not till next morning.

Dennis But then when you did . . .

Lynne Well, then I thought—they'll be coming round to interview me. And I don't just mean me specially—I mean everybody. So I thought, well, wait till somebody comes to interview me and then I'll tell 'em. Only they never did. Police nor nobody. Never came to see either of us, did they?

Dennis No.

Lynne So that were like two or three days had passed and I still hadn't told anybody. And then when I heard Jack's story . . . well, that made me stop and think, didn't it. Because he obviously wasn't mentioning that anybody had called. It was just him and this Philip Mercer. So I thought, well, if he's not mentioning it then . . .

Dennis You thought you wouldn't either.

Lynne Yeah. And then this was getting weeks afterwards, so I thought, well, if I ever do say anything, people are only going to want to know why I didn't speak sooner so . . . I ended up keeping me mouth shut.

Dennis But you saw somebody arrive . . . ?

Lynne Yes.

Maggie Actually there might have been somebody here.

Lynne There was.

Maggie No, I mean . . . I'm agreeing. Because I'd thought I'd heard voices, only I'd persuaded myself I must have been imagining . . .

Dennis Voices . . . ?

Maggie In here. Jack and somebody else talking down here.

Lynne Well then.

Maggie Only I was three-quarters asleep. And then, afterwards, when I heard what Jack was telling the police . . . I thought I must have been dreaming.

Lynne Well, you weren't.

Maggie Well, or else what I'd actually heard was Jack challenging Philip Mercer when he broke in.

Dennis But did it sound like that?

Maggie Not really. It sounded like people talking.

Dennis (*to Lynne*) And are you certain you saw somebody?

Lynne Positive.

Dennis Well then this ... I mean this puts his whole story up the shoot. Everything! All right, Philip Mercer knowing Jack, that's not what you expect ... it's a bit peculiar. But it's nothing to what you two are saying. That there was somebody else in here when Philip Mercer broke in!

Maggie And then what happened?

Dennis God knows.

Lynne Well, yes, he might. But I don't suppose we ever will, will we?

Dennis And Jack knows.

Lynne So?

Dennis So we can ask him.

Lynne Dennis ...

Dennis Oh, politely. We'll ask him politely.

Meanwhile Maggie has been listening intently

Maggie Shhh ... !

Lynne What, love?

Maggie (*listening again; then quietly; indicating towards the kitchen*) There's somebody out there.

A pause as they all listen

Dennis Yeah.

Lynne Oh, God.

Maggie It can't be somebody else breaking in ... ?

Dennis I'll, er ... I'll go and see, shall I ... ?

Lynne Dennis, be careful!

Maggie I'll ring the police.

Dennis Wait. Listen.

They do. A pause as nothing happens. They look fearfully at one another

Then the door is flung open and Jack hurls himself into the room, shotgun at the ready

This provokes screams and cries of alarm from the other three. He swings the gun as though threatening them. They duck and cower away, till he finally lowers it

Jack You're all right? I mean there's nobody ...

Dennis What the hell ... ?

Maggie Jack, what're you doing?

Lynne My heart's going like the clappers.

Jack I'm sorry, I'm sorry. But there's been nobody in here?

Maggie What do you mean?

Dennis *We*'ve been in here.

Jack I mean anybody else? Well, no, obviously not. No, I'm sorry.

Maggie Gone crazy ...

Dennis Yeah, you've joined the SAS now? Storming buildings? Get our lads out at all costs ... ?

Jack Yeah, all right ...

Lynne Whatever he's doing, he's driving me to drink. (*She helps herself to another*)

Jack I just didn't know what I might find when I came in here.

Dennis Like what?

Jack Like anything. There's that car again, that one you saw earlier . . .

Dennis Oh.

Maggie Oh, no.

Jack Yeah.

Maggie Where?

Jack Couple of streets away. Near that filling-station.

Dennis With the same two men in it?

Jack Nobody in it. It's just parked there, empty. Which is why I didn't know what I was going to find when I got back here. But, anyway, I'm sorry if I frightened anybody.

Maggie You did. But you're frightening me more by what you're saying about that car.

Jack Then I'm sorry about that as well. Just forget it.

Maggie But it must mean they're out there again.

Jack Or that their car broke down . . . or that they were never who we thought they were or . . . Look, just forget it. They're not in here—that's all that matters. And I've got the newspapers. So hang on a minute and you're in for a treat.

Jack exits to the kitchen

Maggie They must be out there.

Lynne Well, if they are, then let 'em stay out there. (*To Dennis*) Look, shouldn't we be going?

Dennis In a minute.

Lynne Dennis . . .

Dennis In a minute.

Jack returns with newspapers

Jack Here we are then. What you've all been waiting for. Actually only two had arrived. He reckoned another half-hour and I'd have had the full set, but I knew how eager you all were, didn't want to keep you waiting so . . . First of all we have the *Daily Express*. Popular tabloid, possibly tending to the right, wouldn't you say, Dennis . . . ?

Dennis grunts

Yes, well, anyway . . . page two. Headline. "Jury Acquit Man Who Shot Burglar". No picture, which is a pity but never mind. Quite a long report . . . which I won't bore you with because you know what happened. Oh, except . . . bit here you might like . . . "Mr Lilley, described in court as a successful business man and respectable member of the community". Says it all really. Don't you think, Dennis?

Dennis Definitely.

Jack Oh, and then there's another bit in the what-d'you-call-it . . . comments column, er . . . ?

Maggie Editorial.

Jack Editorial. Editorial. Just at the bottom. Little paragraph. I'll read you this because it's worth hearing. "The jury that yesterday freed Mr Jack Lilley, charged with manslaughter after disarming and then fatally shooting an intruder into his home, deserves three hearty cheers. Mr Lilley acted courageously in defending himself against an armed thug. It was monstrous he should have had to defend himself again in court." Hear, hear. Couldn't agree more. "In refusing to go along with the misguided prosecution, the jury have reaffirmed that an Englishman's home is still his castle and he has every right to defend it." Not bad, eh.

Dennis Wonderful.

Jack Glad you think so, Dennis. You know, I'm going to cut that out and have it framed. And now we have *The Star*. Great newspaper. Voice of the people.

Dennis Which people?

Jack Oh, quite a lot of 'em.

Dennis Probably.

Jack And here we're on page two again. Nearly the full page but for a couple of ads. "Self-Defence Man Gets Off." By Glen Sempers. Hey, that was the character that turned up at the restaurant.

Maggie Don't remind me.

Jack And we have a picture. (*Which he displays*) Here I am smiling, relaxed ... looking half-pissed actually, but I'm sure my fans will understand. It goes on about the trial ... verdict ... Ah, I'll read this bit. You'll like this bit. "His court appearance behind him, Jack celebrated in a fashionable restaurant in the company of his charming girl-friend, Maggie Jones, twenty-four." You see, if you'd only let him take that picture ...

Maggie I'm glad I didn't.

Jack Anyway. " 'I'm over the moon,' said Jack. 'I believe the case is important because it establishes a man's right to defend himself and his possessions. It's time we all fought back against the thugs and villains who are undermining our society. I'd like to think that what I've done will set an example for other people to follow. This is one battle we have got to win.' " Sound like Churchill, don't I.

Dennis Very much.

Jack I told you it'd go down in history, this case. A cause ... cause ... ?

Maggie *Célèbre.*

Jack One of them.

Dennis And that's it, is it?

Jack For now. Till the rest arrive. But don't worry about missing any, Dennis. I'll have photocopies sent round.

Dennis Thanks.

Jack I might have 'em all framed. Make a sort of display in the shop.

Dennis By the way, we've been talking while you were out.

Jack No law against it.

Lynne You mean I've been talking. Talking too much.

A pause

Jack So? What about? Anybody going to tell me?

Dennis We were talking about Philip Mercer. The man you shot.

Jack Oh, yes?

Dennis We were wondering whether you knew him.

Jack Knew him? How do you mean—knew him! I shot him. I didn't have to know him.

Maggie Dennis met him once. And he said he knew you.

Jack Dennis met . . . ?

Maggie Philip Mercer.

Jack Oh, come on. Not bloody *Casablanca* again . . . !

Dennis No . . .

Jack I thought we'd heard the last of that one. I thought, as stories went, it had been relegated to the fairy-tale class had that one!

Dennis It has.

Maggie Dennis used to teach him.

Jack Yeah?

Dennis Yes.

Jack Teach him what? Breaking-and-entering?

Dennis I came across him at College a few years ago. Then last time I met him we got talking and he happened to mention that he knew you.

Jack Did he now.

Dennis Yes.

Maggie So the question is—did you know him?

Jack And the answer is—no, I didn't.

Dennis So how come he said he knew you?

Jack I don't know how come he said he knew me. I don't care how come. All I know about him was that he broke into this house and I shot him. Now *he* might call that a relationship but . . .

Dennis You'd never met him before?

Jack No.

Dennis So why should he say he knew you?

Jack Have to ask him that. And, anyway, we've only got your word he said that, haven't we. And I don't want to be rude Dennis, but your word is just a little bit suspect around here at the moment.

Dennis Have it your own way. I know what he said.

Jack gives a dismissive shake of the head

Maggie Did anybody else call here that night?

A pause

Jack Look, what is this? What's going on?

Maggie The night Philip Mercer was shot, was there a man called here?

Jack Am I being re-tried or what? You should have invited Judge Jeffreys round. Got him to bring his little black cap. He'd have enjoyed this. He'd have been in his element. Jesus.

Lynne It's my fault. I said I thought I saw somebody come to the house.

Jack Well, and you might well have. There were policemen, ambulancemen . . . God knows who.

Maggie Lynne meant before all that.

Jack Yeah?

Lynne Yes.

Jack Well, then Lynne must have been dreaming. Or drunk. Drunk probably.

Lynne Oh, well thank you.

Jack Well, be honest. There are witnesses. And there are witnesses who drink.

Lynne As a matter of fact I wasn't dreaming or drunk and I did see somebody come to this house.

Jack Oh, you were keeping watch, were you? Keeping an eye open, just in case? Now that's thoughtful. I mean that is what good neighbours are all about.

Lynne I'd been working late and I was still up.

Maggie Look, does it matter what she was doing? It's what she saw that matters!

Jack I don't believe this ...

Maggie Was there anybody, Jack?

Jack I go to get some newspapers. I'm gone fifteen, twenty minutes, and what happens when I get back? Our next-door neighbours—one who fantasizes about having me killed, the other who's moving house to get away from me—they seem to have inveigled you into some sort of conspiracy to ... well, I don't know exactly. All I know is I'm suddenly supposed to be a bosom buddy of Philip Mercer. And what else? That there was somebody else here? And did that somebody else kill him? Was that the idea?

Dennis Could be. We didn't get that far.

Jack Oh, I'm sorry. I interrupted you, did I?

Lynne I know I wasn't drunk and I know I wasn't dreaming and I know I did see somebody!

Jack You know, you and your husband must have a whale of a time. Fantasy lives you lead.

Maggie And what about me?

Jack You ... ?

Maggie I heard you down here talking. Down here, I heard voices.

Jack Oh ... !

Maggie I did, Jack. I heard you talking to somebody. Arguing by the sound of it.

Jack So you are joining the lynch-mob then.

Maggie I just want to know the truth.

Jack And I've told you the truth. The real, down-the-line truth. And you will have to live with it.

She can't hold his gaze. She looks away. Jack turns to the other two

But all right. All right. If these are the sort of party games you go in for ... fine by me. I mean I've been cross-examined by professionals. If you still want to have a go, fire away. I'm probably still on oath from this morning, so we can manage without the bible. Which is probably a good thing because I don't think we've got one anyway.

A pause

Come on. Don't be shy. Let's have some penetrating questions. Tie me in knots. Dennis?

Dennis I've already asked you.

Jack If I knew Philip Mercer . . . ?

Dennis Yes.

Jack Ask me again.

Dennis Did you know him?

Jack No. Next question. Lynne.

Lynne Somebody came to this house.

Jack That's not a question.

Lynne I know it's not a question. It's a statement. Statement of fact, because I saw him.

Jack Well, I didn't.

Lynne You answered the door to him.

Jack No.

Lynne Yes, you did. And you can lie till you're blue in the face, it won't alter what I saw.

Jack Well, let me ask you a few questions then. Cross-examine, as we say. Are you saying that this person—who didn't exist, but forget that for now—are you saying that he was here when Philip Mercer broke in?

Lynne Must have been.

Jack And was he still here when the police arrived?

Lynne Apparently not.

Jack Well, then that is a mystery, isn't it. I mean did I sneak him out or spirit him away or what?

Lynne I don't know what you did.

Jack Let's take things a step further. I mean let's not be restricted by the facts or the truth. Let's throw a few ideas around, see what we can come up with. Perhaps he was the one who did the shooting. What do you think?

Lynne shrugs

Well, I quite like the idea. I think it's a goer. He did the shooting, but I insisted on taking the blame. Bit stuck for a motive though, aren't we. I mean why should I do that?

Lynne I've no idea.

Jack Neither have I. Because basically what we've got here is a load of balls. Doesn't make a blind bit of sense, any of it!

Lynne I still say I saw somebody. And I'll go to my grave saying that I saw somebody.

Jack chuckles and shakes his head

Maggie So is it my turn now?

Jack Why not. You're going to ask me about voices? You heard voices?

Maggie shakes her head

No . . . ?

Maggie Oh, I heard voices, yeah.

Jack Mystical experience.

Maggie Might well have been. But I want to ask you about something else. The night it happened, you said you were going out, that there was somebody you had to meet.

Jack shrugs

You did.

Jack If you say so.

Maggie You said you were going to meet him down the club. That you had some business to discuss.

Jack I might well have done. A lot of things were said that night. By both of us.

Maggie Well, yes. Which is why you never actually went. You were planning to but——

Jack OK. OK. So I was going to see a man and I didn't. So?

Maggie So I imagine he was waiting for you.

Jack I imagine he was.

Maggie And then when this club—wherever it was—when this club finally closed and you hadn't turned up . . . well, then he came here.

A pause

Jack Ah.

Lynne And I saw him!

Dennis Makes sense to me.

Jack Oh, smart, yes. Very smart. If there was a prize for this game then you'd have won it, my love. Pity I don't remember a word of all this, but if it makes you happy then you believe it. Why the hell should I care?

Maggie Oh, I think you should care very much, Jack. Because I think I know what happened.

Jack We all know what happened. Anybody who can read the newspapers knows what happened.

Maggie No. No, I don't mean that story you told in court. And I don't mean the story you told me either.

Jack (*a warning*) Which was for your ears only.

Maggie (*nodding*) To keep me here. Make me feel I couldn't ever get away after what you'd done. Because you'd done it all for me, hadn't you. I was supposed to feel responsible for it.

Jack Look, you want to talk about that—we'll talk about it. But, before we do, I think it's time our guests were leaving.

Maggie And me, Jack. Me with them.

Jack Hey, look, game ends, all right? Everybody. I think we're all getting a little rough. Little over-enthusiastic. Even those bastards in court didn't try to chew me up like you people.

Maggie You'd really like to believe it, wouldn't you. All this hero shit. The Englishman defending his three-bedroomed castle.

Jack I said game's over. It's not funny anymore. People are going to get hurt.

They stare at one another for a moment. Then Maggie turns to Lynne

Maggie You know Suzanne, Lynne?

Lynne What, you mean . . . ?

Maggie Jack's second wife.

Jack Hey . . .

Lynne Oh. Course, yeah.

Maggie Well, I met her. On the day Philip Mercer was killed.

Lynne Yeah?

Jack What's this about Suzanne? What do you want to drag her into this for?

Maggie (*ignoring that*) We talked about Jack.

Lynne Well, you would, wouldn't you.

Jack I've told you, Maggie. I'm not amused by any of this anymore.

Maggie And she said something I didn't understand. Or anyway, I didn't take seriously. She said Jack had been lucky to get away with what he had——

Jack Ha.

Maggie Considering the risks he took.

Lynne Yeah?

Jack The biggest of which was marrying that lying cow in the first place.

Maggie She said one day somebody was going to walk into his shop and find they were buying their own property.

Jack Oh, she did? Well, you know what that is? That's slander.

Maggie I thought she was joking.

Jack I'm going to sue the bitch. Get some of my own money back.

Maggie Only she wasn't joking, was she, Jack? You're what they call a fence, aren't you? A fence . . .

Jack I'm what they call soft in the head to stand for this.

Maggie You buy and sell stolen goods.

Jack I'm a respectable business man. Read the newspapers!

Maggie (*resuming, to Lynne*) After I'd talked to Suzanne, I came home. And we ended up having an almighty row because I said I wanted to leave.

Jack Hey, hey, come on . . .

Maggie Which was why Jack didn't go out to meet the man he should have been meeting at the club. I went to bed. And, later on, the man came here, looking for him.

Jack Yeah, we've had that once. It was clever the first time, not so good the second.

Lynne And I saw him.

Maggie You saw him.

Jack Made a film, didn't they. *The Third Man*. Who was he? The mysterious Third Man. I bet you've seen it at your college society, Dennis, eh?

Dennis Yeah.

Jack Yeah, well, I think what we're getting here is a re-make. *Third Man Part Two*.

Maggie Only there was no third man.

Jack No . . . ?

Lynne But I saw——

Maggie I know you did! The man you saw ... was Philip Mercer.

Lynne But he came to the front door.

Maggie Of course he did. Why shouldn't he? He knew Jack. Jack was his fence, weren't you?

Jack I think you should be very careful what you're saying, you know that. I think you should be very, very careful.

Maggie He came here and you let him in. And you argued with him. About money I suppose, was it? Anyway, they were the voices I heard, you arguing with him. And you ended up killing him.

Jack You think so?

Maggie I do, yes.

Jack No, sorry. Way out. You want to know what happened—read the newspapers.

Maggie It was your gun. You've already told me it was your gun.

Dennis It was?

Lynne Oh, my God.

Jack Look, I've been tried and found innocent, OK? British justice, in open court. It's over. Finished. You can tell one another all the fairy stories you like, whatever turns you on, but it doesn't change one iota of what the courts decided or what's written down here. (*He indicates the newspapers*)

Maggie It changes it for me.

Jack Your privilege, darling. But, see, only two people really know what happened in this room. And one's Philip Mercer and he won't be telling anybody. And the other one's me and I've already given my version.

Maggie And you stick to it, Jack. You be happy with it.

Jack I intend to be.

Dennis And what about Mercer's family?

Jack What about 'em?

Dennis They might know as well.

Jack They're a race of degenerates. A sub-species from Fairfields. Who cares what they think?

Dennis Oh, so you do know 'em then?

Jack says nothing

Only this motion of yours that people should take arms to defend themselves. I suppose it stretches to avenging themselves as well? It might be they feel the same way.

A pause

Jack I see. So we've had the evidence. We've had the verdict. Guilty. And now you're passing sentence. Not only passing sentence but deciding on who's going to be the executioners.

Dennis I'm only saying——

Jack And, of course, you're right! Have the courage of your convictions, Dennis. If I am what you all think I am, then why shouldn't they have their chance. That's if they've got the guts to take it. (*He draws back the curtains, opens the french windows and stands before them*)

The others react with dismay

(*Calling*) Anybody out there? Well, come on then. I'm here. Sentenced
and delivered for execution.

And he stands for a long moment. Nothing happens

Lynne Come away . . .
Dennis Yeah, come on, Jack . . .
Jack Your last chance!
Lynne You're just being stupid.
Jack Reprieved. (*And finally he steps away from the window*) Looks like
you'll have to be content without a death.
Lynne We will be.
Maggie And what's that ridiculous performance supposed to prove?
Jack Well I believe it is the custom that if a prisoner survives the gallows
then he's taken to be innocent. He's set free.
Maggie You are free.
Jack I am, yes. Free and innocent. And I still intend to marry you.

*As Lynne moves to close the french windows a rifle shot rings out. She clutches
her chest, gasps, then collapses to the ground. The others stare, horrified*

Dennis Lynne . . .
Jack Stay down, stay down . . . ! (*Rushing to the window*) Dennis, give me
the gun.

*Dennis picks up the gun, moves as though to give it to Jack but then stops. He
is pointing it at him. Jack stares*

Dennis.

*He moves round but Dennis swings the gun to cover him. For a moment Jack
pleads*

No . . .

But it's Maggie who moves to take the gun from Dennis

Maggie Give it to me. Dennis, give it to me.

So Dennis hands over the gun, then moves away to Lynne

Jack (*relieved*) Give it to me. There's a good girl.

*But she pulls the trigger. He catches the full force of the shot, falls. Then she
puts down the gun, moves to the phone, dials 999 as we begin fade to Black-out*

Maggie (*on the phone*) Police.

CURTAIN

FURNITURE AND PROPERTY LIST

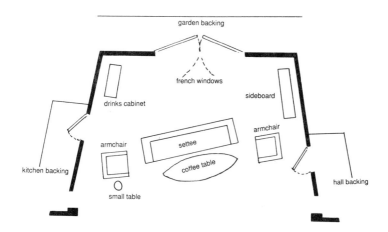

ACT I

On stage: Settee
Armchairs
Coffee table
Drinks cabinet. *In it:* glasses, bottles of drink including brandy, gin, tonic,
  beer
Sideboard. *On it:* ashtray, table lamp
Small table. *On it:* table lamp
Curtains at french windows (open)
Carpet
Other furniture and dressing as required

Off stage: Packet of cigarettes, lighter **(Lynne)**
Packet of cigarettes **(Dennis)**
Plate of sandwiches **(Maggie)**
Shotgun **(Jack)**—required twice

Personal: **Jack:** wrist-watch ⎫ required throughout
Dennis: wrist-watch ⎭

ACT II

Off stage: Cigarettes and lighter **(Dennis)**
Shotgun **(Jack)**
2 newspapers **(Jack)**

Personal: **Lynne, Jack:** concealed blood sacs

LIGHTING PLOT

Practical fittings required: wall brackets, 2 table lamps

Interior. A living-room. The same scene throughout

ACT I   Night

To open: Room in darkness; starry sky outside

ACT II   Night

To open: As end Act I before Black-out

EFFECTS PLOT

ACT I

Cue 16   **Lynne** moves to close french windows   (Page 54)
           Rifle shot

Cue 17   **Maggie** pulls trigger   (Page 54)
           Shotgun blast

MADE AND PRINTED IN GREAT BRITAIN BY
LATIMER TREND & COMPANY LTD PLYMOUTH
MADE IN ENGLAND